Day by Day with God

September–December 2003

DAY BY DAY
WITH GOD

Bible Readings for Women

SEPTEMBER–DECEMBER 2003

Christina Press
BRF
Tunbridge Wells/Oxford

The Bible Reading Fellowship,
First Floor, Elsfield Hall, 15–17 Elsfield Way, Oxford OX2 8FG

First published in Great Britain 2003

ISBN 1 84101 229 7

Jacket design: JAC Design for Print, Crowborough

Trade representation in UK:
Lion Publishing plc, Mayfield House, 256 Banbury Road
Oxford OX2 7DH

Distributed in Australia by:
Willow Connection, PO Box 288, Brookvale, NSW 2100.
Tel: 02 9948 3957; Fax: 02 9948 8153;
E-mail: info@willowconnection.com.au

Distributed in New Zealand by:
Scripture Union Wholesale, PO Box 760, Wellington
Tel: 04 385 0421; Fax: 04 384 3990; E-mail: suwholesale@clear.net.nz

Distributed in South Africa by:
Struik Book Distributors, PO Box 193, Maitland 7405
Tel: 021 551 5900; Fax: 021 551 1124; E-mail: enquiries@struik.co.za

Acknowledgments

Scriptures from The New Revised Standard Version of the Bible,
Anglicized Edition, copyright © 1989, 1995 by the Division of
Christian Education of the National Council of the Churches of
Christ in the USA, used by permission. All rights reserved.

Scripture quotations taken from *The Holy Bible, New International
Version*, copyright © 1973, 1978, 1984 by International Bible Society.
Used by permission of Hodder & Stoughton Ltd. All rights reserved.
'NIV' is a registered trademark of International Bible Society. UK
trademark number 1448790.

Scriptures quoted from the Good News Bible published by The Bible
Societies/HarperCollins Publishers Ltd, UK © American Bible Society
1966, 1971, 1976, 1992, used with permission.

The Living Bible copyright © 1971 by Tyndale House Publishers.

Extracts from the Authorized Version of the Bible (The King James
Bible), the rights in which are vested in the Crown, are reproduced by
permission of the Crown's Patentee, Cambridge University Press.

Printed in Great Britain by Bookmarque, Croydon

Contents

The Editor writes...

Life is full of changes and challenges! Two years ago, my husband retired and we moved to a different part of the country. Since then, we have enjoyed living in our own home and are constantly thanking God for his goodness to us. We are fit, we have made new friends and there is plenty to do. In fact, there is more than enough to do, and I became sure that the time had come for me to retire as Editor of *Day by Day with God*.

It has been great to work with such a wonderful team of writers, along with all those at BRF who answer my queries and make sure that the material sent in ends up as the book you read. It's quite a long process, producing each issue of *Day by Day with God*. It takes at least fifteen months from the original planning through to each issue being ready to go out to you—so when you read this issue, I will actually have been retired for over a year.

New Editor

I am very pleased to be able to introduce you to your new Editor, Catherine Butcher. She has already planned the issues for 2004 and will, I am sure, enjoy hearing from you as much as I have in the past.

Catherine has been editing and writing for a number of years. She trained as a journalist and is now working towards an MA in Christian Spirituality at the University of London. She has edited *Woman Alive*, *Renewal* and a number of consumer magazines. She publishes *The Christian Counsellor* and writes for *Christianity & Renewal* magazine. As well as ghost-writing a numer of books, she has written a children's book, *Daniel and the Dark Arts*, under the pseudonym of Earnest Spellbinder.

A Scot by birth, she now lives in Eastbourne with her husband Adrian, a BBC news journalist, and her two junior school-aged children. Catherine is also actively involved in her church and local community. So I am quite sure that *Day by Day with God* is going to be in good hands.

A privilege

It has been a privilege to have been the Editor for the past six years and I have learnt so much about the way God strengthens and guides us when we are asked to do something that seems daunting. There have been many times when things have gone wrong as I have been working on the copy: my computer has broken down, or notes have not arrived as expected, and I have got into a total panic about getting everything ready on time. There have been occasions when I have ended up with two notes on the same passage by different writers for the same issue, or else there has not been enough copy for the Magazine section—and yet, when each issue has been completed, I have been able to thank God wholeheartedly for his guiding hand and his calming reassurance that everything would come together in time and that the content would help those who read the pages to see how God is with them in their daily lives.

Chosen

As I finish this particular work with *Day by Day with God*, one verse from the Bible has been going round and round inside my head. They are the words of Jesus, 'You did not choose me but I chose you' (John 15:16). We can go through life feeling that we make all the decisions about what we do, where we live, who we love. Of course we do have to use our own initiative, but the most important issue is knowing that we are God's chosen people, his children. So wherever we are, whatever we do, whatever changes happen to our circumstances, one thing stays the same: we are his children living in his world, ready to do whatever seems right in his name.

Thanks be to God.

Mary Reid

Contributors

Beryl Adamsbaum is a former language teacher living in France. She is involved in teaching, translating and preaching.

Diana Archer is a writer and editor, and has three teenage children. Starting a church in her lounge with her husband Graham, an Anglican vicar, led to her writing *Who'd Plant a Church?* (Christina Press), a warts-and-all account of church and vicarage life. She now works with the Damaris Trust in Southampton, producing Connect Bible studies.

Anne Coomes has been a journalist for the Church of England for nearly twenty years. Together with the well-known artist Taffy Davies, she has launched www.parishpump.co.uk, a website providing articles for parish magazine editors. Anne also does freelance communications work for various dioceses, and has written five books. She holds a degree in theology and is Reader for her parish in north Cheshire.

Molly Dow has a degree in chemistry and a diploma in theology. She is a Church of England Reader and is the Spiritual Direction Adviser for Carlisle Diocese. She has edited and co-written several courses on prayer, is the author of *Mountains and Molehills*, and is married to Graham, the Bishop of Carlisle.

Rosemary Green has left the staff of Wycliffe Hall, Oxford, in order to have more time for ten grandchildren and for her local parish. She continues to be involved with *Women in Mission*, and she loves writing for BRF, trying to make the Bible alive and relevant in a world that is increasingly ignorant of this book.

Margaret Killingray is a tutor at the London Institute for Contemporary Christianity. She has assisted Dr John Stott and others in running Christian Impact conferences here and overseas. Margaret and her husband, David, have three daughters and five grandchildren.

Jennifer Rees Larcombe, one of Britain's best-loved Christian authors and speakers, lives in Kent. She contributes regularly to Christian magazines, including a problem page, and has recently published a book on the ministry of angels, a children's Bible story-book and an account of her dramatic recovery, *Unexpected Healing*. Her latest book for BRF is *Beauty from Ashes*.

Chris Leonard, her husband and two student-age children live in Surrey. Chris has a degree in English and theology and her twelve books range from biography and devotional to children's stories. She enjoys leading creative writing workshops because 'people are so interesting—and they grow!' Recent BRF publications include *The Heart of Christmas* and *The Road to Easter* (co-written with Jacqui Gardner).

Mary Reid is the Editor of *Day by Day with God*. She has been a secretary, primary school teacher, special needs co-ordinator, school governor and a magazine and book editor. Her husband has recently retired from being the Bishop of Maidstone; they have three children and four grandchildren.

Alie Stibbe is a freelance writer and translator who has contributed regularly to *Renewal* and other Christian magazines. Her recent work includes *Word Bytes—a completely manageable Bible* (BRF 2003), 365 devotional readings for teenagers, translated from Norwegian. She has just embarked on a PhD in Scandinavian Studies at University College London, focusing on the devotional literature of the late 18th century revival in Norway. Alie is married to Mark Stibbe, Vicar of St Andrew's, Chorleywood. They have four children aged 6–14.

**Contributors are identified by their initials
at the bottom of each page.**

A Morning Prayer

Thank you, heavenly Father,
for this new day.
Be with me now
in all I do
and think
and say,
that it will be to your glory.

Amen

Flight

Yet man is born to trouble as surely as sparks fly upward.

What does 'flight' mean to you? That particular noun has two verbs—are you flying (high) or fleeing (from trouble)? Are you an optimist whose glass is half full, or anxious because it's half empty? Perhaps it was having to live with a name like Eliphaz the Temanite that turned Job's 'comforter' into the worst kind of judgmental pessimist. Eliphaz's words, quoted above, were hardly what Job needed to hear when he'd just lost his livelihood, servants, house, sons and daughters in one day, then discovered his own body covered with painful sores!

I'm naturally a pessimistic worrier, which doesn't chime well with my Christian faith. Isaiah 40:22 says that God 'sits enthroned above the circle of the earth'. He invites us to soar high with him, getting a God's-eye perspective on mundane or even horrific difficulties on earth. Spending time with God, reading his word, then letting him 'read' us and speak to us often enables him to impart *shalom* (peace/wholeness). Far better than a good massage, his love smooths away our tension.

God is utterly secure in himself but he's not sitting around, convinced that all is perfect in the best of all possible worlds. He sees what is really going on—neither optimist, nor pessimist, God's a realist! Over the next couple of weeks we'll explore some reality around the fleeing, as well as the flapping/soaring kind of flight. Even Jesus had to flee into Egypt. The Bible reminds us how time, material security and life itself all fly away. The good news is that, although 'even youths grow tired and weary, and young men stumble and fall', God gets involved, promising, 'but those who hope in the Lord will renew their strength. They will soar on wings like eagles; they will run and not grow weary, they will walk and not be faint' (Isaiah 40:30–31).

Whether we are pessimistic flee-ers or optimistic high fly-ers, Lord, help us make truths from your word reality in our lives.

CL

Flights of worship

'Does the hawk take flight by your wisdom and spread his wings towards the south?'

God is answering Job's complaints. Speaking from out of a mighty storm he shows his power, then points out that he made the swiftest, the strongest, the highest—creatures that we can't even begin to understand. Job's moans about his own unjust suffering seem puny. Greatness is one aspect of God which we forget at our peril. Who are we to answer him back, to question him, to nag him as though his timing should be our timing? God has dreamt up all the wonders of this world, including us human beings. Before him we are nothing—except that he has called us his children and the apple of his eye! He also calls us friends but he's not our equal; he is majestic; he is King; he is on the throne.

And we, we can dissect animals to find out how they work— when they are dead. Scientists can use computer power to begin to unravel DNA but can't create life. Igniting fossil fuel, we can jet through the air; we can hang from a parachute, glide in a glider— but we ourselves can't fly. We can reach for the stars, count them, find out facts about them—but we didn't make them. We didn't dream up the wide-winged albatross or the condor soaring effort-less above the widest oceans or highest mountains, nor the swift's high-speed sleeping-on-the-wing. When young birds migrate across continents for the first time without help from their parents, we have no idea how they do it. Mysteries remain. Only God knows. We're wise to let him be God. We're wiser still to let him be himself in us—or maybe foolish because who knows what might happen?

Think of all the things you see around which are God's amazing flights of fancy. Spend some time in wonder, worshipping him.

CL

Divine wings

*The priests then brought the ark of the Lord's covenant to its place
in the inner sanctuary of the temple, the Most Holy Place, and
put it beneath the wings of the cherubim. The cherubim spread
their wings over the place of the ark and overshadowed the ark
and its carrying poles.*

The gold wings of the two cherubim, according to 1 Kings 6, were
huge, touching the sides of the room and meeting over the ark in
the middle. Resting beneath them, the ark-box, held in awe as the
visible presence of God, contained simply the two tablets of the law.
I wonder if the golden wings at the most sacred heart of the temple
are the source of the picture of God sheltering us beneath his wings?
It occurs so many times throughout the scriptures.

Those wings, arching over us, give shelter and warmth, but also
freedom, because God isn't confined to a box, to tablets of stone or
to a room; he's not earthbound. He is Spirit, and Old Testament
writers sometimes expressed this in terms of flight. Psalm 18:10 says,
'He mounted the cherubim and flew; he soared on the wings of the
wind.' What a wonderful picture! And if he can fly in this way, so
can we. Jesus said, 'The wind blows wherever it pleases. You hear its
sound, but you cannot tell where it comes from or where it is going.
So it is with everyone born of the Spirit' (John 3:8).

I don't mean people can fly, literally—though maybe we'll be able
to in heaven! But when you do something which is clearly not in your
own strength but in his, doesn't it feel a bit like flying—dizzy-making,
exhilarating but somehow safe too, because the powerful wing-beats
are his?

---

*Meditate on that beautiful verse from Psalm 63: 'Because you are my
help, I sing in the shadow of your wings'—and fly with him.*

CL

Pigs might fly!

'They will come trembling like birds from Egypt, like doves from Assyria. I will settle them in their homes,' declares the Lord.

First of all the Lord tells his prophet Hosea to marry a well-known adulteress—and take on her children too. Hosea learns the pain of loving someone who is unfaithful. Through the prophet's highly charged words, God makes clear his own anger and hurt at Israel's unfaithfulness. Like Hosea's wife, Gomer, Israel hasn't been unfaithful once or twice. She's made it a lifestyle, running after the gods and power of Assyria and Egypt, breaking covenant vows between herself and her God. But after God's thunderous threats of total destruction come some of the most sublime words of healing and unending love ever written—do read them.

Recently a TV programme featured a class of secondary school children, reunited for the first time since 1977. Apart from their drama teacher, most staff thought little of them. The bright kids had gone to another school. Most of this group played truant, got into various kinds of trouble and finished their education with, at best, one 'O' level or CSE.

As adults, though, they appeared likeable, lively, responsible people. Not until the final credits rolled did we see one had become a Hollywood casting director, another a top sales executive. Most surprising of all, the school rebel is now a Methodist minister. The programme ended with a shot of him preaching the gospel!

Israel still messed up after God had chosen her, believed in her, given her ten-thousand-and-one chances. That proves we can choose not to accept his grace. He won't *make* us fly, or fly back. But he does love us to bits. Like that drama teacher who, in a couple of years, influenced those kids for good, God does believe in us. With him it's almost as though the more piggish and lumbering we are, the more we root about in the dirt and don't look at the sky, the more he says, 'Come on, let's fly!'

Praise the God of grace!

CL

Flying away from God

If I rise on the wings of the dawn, if I settle on the far side of the sea, even there your hand will guide me, your right hand will hold me fast.

I was old enough to know better when something at church upset me so much that I spiralled right downwards, concluding that Christianity didn't work. Maybe I needed to change my religion, I announced to my church house-group leader and his wife. They weren't in the least shocked.

He smiled and said, 'Well, Chris, if you're set on becoming a Buddhist, would you like us to help shave your head?' I started to laugh then. I'd been as silly as my diminutive four-year-old daughter who would occasionally get cross with us, stamp her foot and announce she was going to 'hit the road'. My offers to help pack her bag and hints about needing more than her pillow and pink crocodile never failed to restore calm and hugs. She didn't love 'the road'—she loved us, just as I didn't love (or know anything about) Buddha; I loved Jesus.

My house-group leader knew me nearly as well as I knew my daughter—but the psalm says the Lord knows us better than anyone else. 'For you created my inmost being; you knit me together in my mother's womb' (v. 13). We can do all kinds of daft things, even try to run away from God. But he knows us—the good in us and the bad—so he's never disillusioned with us. And he's everywhere, even in the darkness, the psalm says. Even in the darkness of our blackest moods he specializes in turning darkness into light.

I do manage to fly away from him sometimes, usually into busyness. Or I try flying to him and he doesn't _appear_ to be around. That's the time to cling on to promises like, 'I will never leave you nor forsake you' (Joshua 1:5). They are true.

Lord, we pray for those who are running away from you and those who are trying to find you.

CL

Betrayal-flight

*Oh that I had the wings of a dove! I would fly away
and be at rest.*

David is in anguish—his thoughts deeply troubled. He fears his
enemy's taunts more because the enmity is coming from his once-
close friend, with whom he enjoyed 'sweet fellowship as we walked
with the throng at the house of God'. No wonder David wants to fly
away and be at rest, to escape from his responsibilities as leader of
his people and become like a dove, free to go at any time.

It's a terrible thing, betrayal, especially if the betrayer is a close
Christian friend. It happens. A partner suddenly walks out of what
appears to be a good Christian marriage; someone turns against a
fellow Christian colleague and ruins his business; a revered spiritual
leader sparks pain and division within a Christian organization.

As well as causing anguish, betrayals like these can make us doubt
ourselves, can spoil good memories and trigger depression, can pre-
vent us from trusting ourselves or others again—all of which com-
pounds the damage. David is very honest about the devastation this
particular betrayal wrought in him, but in the end he refuses the
dove's option—to fly away. Instead, as so often in the psalms, he
finds a new perspective: 'Cast your cares on the Lord and he will
sustain you'. Yes, this is where one of the most-quoted verses in the
Bible comes from! I guess if we don't experience overwhelming cares,
anguish and betrayal, if we aren't ever in the pits, we never prove the
truth of those words. Two things are for sure: David didn't write
them glibly, and he ends the psalm not with the resolution of his
problem but by saying, 'As for me, I trust in (God).'

---

*Lord, we pray for those who are going through the anguish of betrayal.
May they, like David, refuse to run away but bring their pain to you
instead. May they come to a place where they can trust you and find
your road towards healing.*

                                                                    CL

16

Flying in the face of danger

Boaz replied, 'I've been told all about what you have done for your mother-in-law since the death of your husband—how you left your father and mother and your homeland and came to live with a people you did not know before... May you be richly rewarded by... the God of Israel, under whose wings you have come to take refuge.'

If a trained hawk becomes irritated with its master, sometimes it will fly in his face—that's the origin of the phrase, 'flying in the face of danger'. Sometimes, as Christians, we need to fly in the face not of our Master, but of our internal enemies—whether those be fear, laziness, rejection, jealousy, unforgiveness or whatever.

Ruth's enemy wasn't sin but bereavement. In those days, to be widowed had even more serious and difficult consequences than it does today. Ruth could have lived with her Moabite kin but she was determined to stay with her Jewish mother-in-law, bitter Naomi, whose two sons had died. Flying away from the comfort of the familiar and into the face of danger, anxiety and convention, Ruth insisted on accompanying Naomi back to Israel, swearing not to leave until death parted them. Naomi's people would become her people, Naomi's God her God. Bold, grieving Ruth found not danger but shelter and protection with Naomi's people Israel—especially with husband-to-be Boaz and with Naomi's God.

Ruth didn't know it, but the image of God sheltering people like chicks under his wings occurs again and again in the Bible. Chicks have to leave the nest and venture abroad, finding food for themselves—but, if danger threatens, they rush to shelter under their parents' wings. We dare fly in the face of our enemies only because we have an even more secure place in God.

Help us to nestle close beneath your wings, Lord—so that, when necessary, we'll have the strength to be like small birds flying in the face of something big and powerful which appears to have mastery over us.

CL

Manslaughter-flight

A man may... swing his axe to fell a tree, the head may fly off and hit his neighbour and kill him. That man may flee to one of these cities and save his life.

Here are both fleeing and flying, in one verse! God commanded Israel to set up three cities of refuge in the promised land. In the days of an 'eye for an eye', a life for a life, these cities served as refuges for any who committed what we might call 'manslaughter'. They were humanely advanced in those vengeful days, but surely our legal system has manslaughter sorted now. Why study this quaint old scripture?

Well, someone who visited our church last year believed God wanted us to act as a 'city of refuge'. As we tested her words, this obscure passage from Deuteronomy became well-thumbed. What could it mean for us in a nice Surrey village, today? There are some delightful people in our church—and a distinct lack of cheating tax-men, prostitutes and the kind of rough types known as 'sons of thunder' who hung around Jesus. Yet our local paper reports drug and alcohol-related crime and vandalism. Taxi drivers are refusing to pick up fares from the station at night because of violent attacks. Local police keep uncovering paedophile and pornography rings. How would we cope as a church if such 'menaces to society' found Jesus? Though the Holy Spirit often works dramatic transformations, people emerging from chaotic or evil lifestyles face huge challenges; they'd need strong support. As for manslaughter, there are many business people here, working for multi-nationals. It's a moral maze out there. I wonder how many experience guilt, having been involved in making decisions which later have adversely affected whole areas in developed or developing countries?

Father, of course your church is a city of refuge—we're all transgressors who deserve to die. Help us to reach out to other people who need the refuge only you can give. Help us to see people through Jesus' eyes.

CL

Fly-away time and money

Cast but a glance at riches and they are gone, for they will surely sprout wings and fly off to the sky like an eagle.

My daughter and I agree—she cannot be old enough for university. Either some sci-fi black hole has stolen years or time really does fly. Where else could 19 years go? 'The length of our days is seventy years… they quickly pass and we fly away' Psalm 90 says, then asks, 'Teach us to number our days aright, that we may gain a heart of wisdom… Satisfy us in the morning with your unfailing love, that we may sing for joy and be glad all our days.'

Money flies too, not only for students. Take pensions. Fraud or mismanagement has destroyed certain pension funds, while local authorities, discovering theirs are under-funded, want our council tax payments to make up the shortfall for their employees. Financial pundits say that, with life expectancy much increased and care-homes ever more expensive, few of us are making enough provision for our old age. Meanwhile insurance costs rocket and the NHS fights a losing battle to fulfil its pledge to look after us 'from the cradle to the grave'. Worrying, isn't it?

Britain is a prosperous country. Despite lacking sufficient food, fuel and/or shelter, compared with much of the world, our poorest live in luxury. But even the better off are affected when the stock market plummets, business bubbles burst, housing costs rise and people's grown-up children can't afford homes. The ancient proverb still applies. Riches still have a habit of vanishing over the horizon as suddenly as a bird. That's probably why the previous verse says, 'Do not wear yourself out to get rich; have the wisdom to show restraint.' There's not a lot of point killing ourselves to get (or stay) even comfortably off. Better to trust God.

We pray for all those trapped by poverty, in the developed as well as the developing world, for those with serious money worries, especially young adults and those approaching old age.

CL

Flights of locusts

You have increased the number of your merchants till they are
more than the stars of the sky, but like locusts they strip the land
and then fly away.

I bet there aren't many sermons or Bible reading notes on Nahum!
You'll find it just after Micah, towards the end of the Old Testa-
ment. This seventh-century poet-prophet was contemporary with
Zephaniah, Habakkuk and Jeremiah. All three chapters of his book
prophesy against Nineveh, the cruel and exploitative capital of the
Assyrian empire—then super-power of the ancient world. Nahum
foretells its humiliating destruction—and indeed it did fall, to the
Babylonians, in 612BC.

So, this is ancient history—and yet 'the more things change, the
more they stay the same'. Merchants multiplying like swarms of
locusts, stripping the land bare then flying away sounds all too
familiar. Ranchers fell trees, creating grazing for 'beefburgers' until
hooves turn forest to desert, whereupon they move on, leaving
local people without a livelihood. Multi-nationals decide that some
huge area will grow, say, coffee, glutting the market, dropping the
price. Local people have to buy foodstuffs that they always grew
before, increasing their country's debt.

Not all that flies around the globe has the grace of a tern or
swallow. A locust, like some giant grasshopper, is harmless, even
slightly comical, until breeding conditions are right, after which
they swarm together like living clouds, devouring huge tracts of
land. There's nothing wrong with trade, but something has gone
very wrong with our world. What can we do to see the 'breeding
conditions' change? Buy fairly traded goods, write to politicians…?
Above all, pray…

Lord, we pray for the 'merchants', the business and financial people
of our land—may righteousness, not greed, prevail. We pray also for
the leaders of our nation, that they might have wisdom and your way
of looking at all these complexities. Thank you for your strong concern
with economics and poverty. May your economic will be done in our
lives and right across this troubled planet.

                                                            CL

Phoenix rising

After forty days Noah opened the window he had made in the ark and sent out a raven, and it kept flying back and forth until the water had dried up from the earth. Then he sent a dove...

I am writing this on 11 September 2002 as my television flashes back to terrified, bewildered faces of people filmed during the attacks on the World Trade Center. Live pictures of the various anniversary services show the ongoing grief, trauma and quiet courage of survivors, the bereaved, fire-fighters and 'ordinary' people.

In the ancient story of the great flood, 'every living thing on the face of the earth was wiped out,' says Genesis 7:23, even the birds of the air. Only those in the ark were left. Not a pretty tale of two-by-two giraffes—this is unimaginable trauma.

Once the rain stopped, the waters receded steadily until the ark grounded, high on Mount Ararat. Opening a window in the ark, Noah released the two birds. The weaker, gentler dove, unable to land, returned. Noah 'reached out his hand and took the dove and brought it back to himself in the ark'. What a moving detail! Noah dared to release hope in the form of two of the precious lives remaining in the ark—and showed tenderness to the weaker, even when hope seemed barren.

After seven days he released the dove again and it brought back 'a freshly plucked olive leaf'. After another seven days it returned no more. Only then did traumatized Noah remove 'the covering from the ark and see that the surface of the earth was dry'. His whole world had changed; he hadn't dared look before. We know that fertile earth and a rainbowed promise from God awaited him.

Thank you, Lord, that you created the human spirit with capacity for flights of extraordinary hope in terrible circumstances. We pray for all those in trauma, that something eternal that you've put in them may rise bird-like from the ashes and soar to heights where they can see new ways forward.

CL

Flights to, and from, Egypt

'You yourselves have seen what I did to Egypt, and how I carried you on eagles' wings and brought you to myself. Now if you obey me fully and keep my covenant, then out of all nations you will be my treasured possession. Although the whole earth is mine, you will be for me a kingdom of priests and a holy nation.'

I have just re-read J.R.R. Tolkien's *The Lord of the Rings* and this passage reminds me of two weary hobbits being rescued on eagle's wings from what they think is the end of everything.

Joseph fled from murder by his brothers to slavery in the ungodly super-power of Egypt—and there God blessed him. His family joined him later, as beggars, fleeing from famine. Years afterwards the soon-to-be nation of Israel flew out of Egypt's dreadful oppression on the eagle's wings of God's power. Having come through the miraculous parting of waters and the desert, they received a promise—that they could be God's 'most treasured possession'—and a role as a 'kingdom of priests and holy nation'.

Only Jesus would fulfil that role perfectly. Yet, after the worshipping magi inadvertently told the murderous false-king Herod that a new king had been born in Bethlehem, an angel warned Joseph to fly *to* Egypt with Mary and the baby Jesus. Matthew 2:13–15 says this was to fulfil the prophecy, 'Out of Egypt I called my son' (Hosea 11:1). We too have been rescued from 'Egypt'—from oppression, from slavery (to sin). We too have been 'carried on eagle's wings', miraculously, to God himself. We too are his 'treasured possession', his 'sons'—and daughters! And as we acknowledge his lordship fully, he gives us a role and a purpose, dear to his own heart. All of us have a flying hope and a future in him.

You might like to meditate on being borne on eagles' wings. Then take a bird's eye view of yourself and your church as part of the whole amazing story of salvation history.

CL

Healing wings, wings of the sun

But for you who revere my name, the sun of righteousness will rise with healing in its wings. And you will go out and leap like calves released from the stall.

Malachi prophesied these words at a time when the arrogant seemed blessed, when people disobeyed God with impunity. One consequence was that those who tried to follow God were questioning him. God replies that judgment is coming, but also healing, for those who turn to him.

Do Malachi's words sound familiar? I've sung them blithely, as part of that wonderful carol, 'Hark the herald angels sing'—and failed to understand their meaning. I suppose I imagined Jesus the Son coming in glory, like some kind of superior, winged archangel. But the words say 'sun' not 'Son'—and how can a sun have wings? I've looked up various commentaries which all explain that the 'wings' of the sun are its rays. What a beautiful picture—warm rays of sunlight, travelling across the earth, bringing warmth, light and healing.

I had just read the commentaries when we were driving through the southern part of London. At times the road took us high over the North Downs, and we looked down on the great basin over which the conurbation spreads. On that clear evening, a drama of dark clouds painted the wide sky. Through them passed rays of sunlight, which really did resemble wings, now I came to look at them. I found myself praying from this passage and from Isaiah 60:18–19.

Oh Lord, may there be less arrogance and more who revere your name. Be our sun. Bring healing. May violence no longer be heard in our land, nor ruin or destruction within our borders. We long for your salvation and praise. More than for the sun we know, we long for the Lord to be our everlasting light, and for our God to be our glory.

CL

Songs of deliverance

Let my cry come before you, O Lord; give me understanding according to your word. Let my supplication come before you; deliver me according to your promise.

The only trouble with suggesting topics for devotional notes is that you invariably end up being asked to write on one of those particular topics! 'Songs of deliverance' was one such suggestion, made not really knowing quite what a 'song of deliverance' was, only that I liked the bit in Psalm 32:7 where the term originates.

What then is a 'song of deliverance'? It's not the happy sound I make when the postman delivers my long overdue mail order parcel, but a song that celebrates release or rescue, usually from moral corruption or evil. The word 'deliverance' comes from the Latin verb *deliberare* which literally means 'to free from'. Songs of deliverance are therefore songs of salvation, songs that are sung in overwhelming response to what God has saved us from.

When you look for songs of deliverance in the Bible, you find that there aren't many that weren't written by King David, and most are in the Old Testament.

It seems to me that 'songs of deliverance' were not just songs written about salvation from past events, but songs that were pregnant with hope in the promise that the people of Israel would one day be delivered by the promised Messiah. 'Deliver me according to your promise… I long for your salvation' we read in today's passage. There is a long term yearning in these words, as well as an immediate plea.

This yearning of our soul has been met in Jesus Christ; the promise of salvation has been fulfilled. But the immediate plea still speaks to us, reassuring us that our hopes and fears are part of normal everyday human experience. The God who is the same yesterday, today and for ever is still faithful to meet us in those places of difficulty and pain, and the joy of being rescued can still be ours to celebrate.

We can often be so very self-reliant. Spend some time thinking of the things you need saving from so that your heart can sing.

AS

The song of Moses and Miriam

The Lord is my strength and my might, and he has become my salvation; this is my God, and I will praise him, my father's God and I will exalt him. The Lord is a warrior; the Lord is his name... In your steadfast love you led the people whom you redeemed; you guided them by your strength to your holy abode.

The very first song of deliverance that we find in the Bible is the song that Moses and the Israelites sang to the Lord on the banks of the Red Sea. They had been trapped between the sea and Pharaoh's advancing army, and cried out to the Lord in great fear. Moses told them not to be afraid, to stand firm and see the deliverance of the Lord (Exodus 14:13). The Lord would fight for them; they had only to keep still (14:14).

The Israelites were in an apparently impossible situation, but what strikes me is that they only had to keep still. The Lord had brought them that far, and it was unlikely he would abandon them after all he had done and everything they had already been through. The temptation to run must have been overwhelming—but where to?

Life often presents us with situations where there is no apparent way out of a difficulty, and we easily succumb to running round in ever-decreasing circles. Eventually the Lord stops us and reminds us he has promised to fight for us—we have only to be still. 'In returning and rest you shall be saved; in quietness and trust shall be your strength' (Isaiah 30:15). There is no point 'fleeing on horses' because our circumstances will overcome us (Isaiah 30:16).

If we stop and are still long enough to hand our situation to the Lord and wait for him to act, then he will show us the way of deliverance. The path may not be easy—for the Israelites it was a muddy sea-bed—but it leads to a place of celebration, safe from things that threaten to overtake us.

Who is like you, majestic in holiness, awesome in splendour, doing wonders? (v. 11).

AS

The song of Deborah and Barak

'Hear, O kings; give ear, O princes; to the Lord I will sing, I will make melody to the Lord, the God of Israel... To the sound of musicians at the watering-places, there they repeat the triumphs of the Lord, the triumphs of his peasantry in Israel... So perish all your enemies, O Lord! But may your friends be like the sun as it rises in its might.'

Who, you might ask, were Deborah and Barak? After Joshua, Moses' successor, died, the people of Israel were governed by a series of judges. They helped lead the people back to the Lord during the many times that they turned to worshipping foreign gods. Deborah is well known as a woman who had a role as a prophet, judge, and the leader of an army—quite a role model, even by today's standards! I have given you two chapters to read today, to give some background on Deborah and what she did, so that you can better understand the song of deliverance that she sang.

The song of Deborah and Barak is not as well known as the other songs of deliverance in the Old Testament. This is probably because it is less poetic and metaphorical than Moses' and Miriam's song, and therefore more difficult to relate to our own contemporary experience. Their song is more of a direct account of the events of Sisera's defeat and it praises the actions of Deborah and Jael. However, the whole song is threaded through with the glory being given to the Lord (vv. 3, 11 and 31).

We may think a list of military manoeuvres is of no relevance to us, however, it teaches us the value of recalling and recounting the good and great things the Lord has done for us. Today the epic storytelling tradition of the Old Testament has been replaced by personal testimony. Have you got a testimony to share? Think about what the Lord has faithfully brought you through over the years.

If you will go with me I will go; but if you will not go with me, I will not go (Judges 4:8b).

AS

The song of Hannah

My heart exults in the Lord; my strength is exalted in my God… I rejoice in my victory. There is no Holy One like the Lord, no one besides you; there is no Rock like our God. Talk no more so very proudly, let not arrogance come from your mouth; for the Lord is a God of knowledge, and by him actions are weighed.

Hannah was a key character in the history of Israel. The child that the Lord granted her became the last of the judges, the first of the great prophets and the one who anointed the first king over Israel. All this through one woman's desperation, dependence and deliverance. Take some time to acquaint yourself with Hannah's story and the song she sang.

As women, we can all probably identify to some extent with the gamut of emotions that Hannah experienced. Yet in the storm that was her life, Hannah knew that the Lord was as dependable as a rock; rather than retreating into bitterness, she presented herself before the Lord in her distress. She knew it was better to pour out her tears and her heart before the Lord than allow her feelings to stagnate within her.

I have often wondered whether Hannah understood all the implications of the plea and the promise she made to God. Although children were weaned quite late in those days, and Hannah had surely prepared herself and her child, leaving Samuel with Eli the priest must have been heart-rending all round. But she was faithful to her promise.

Hannah's song is a song of personal deliverance rather than of national deliverance. The voice of her critic, Peninnah, had been silenced (2:3) and her own situation had been turned upside down. We know that bitterness, anger and lack of forgiveness grieve the Holy Spirit, but like Hannah, we can pour our hearts out to the Lord and receive healing and deliverance if we choose to do so. Only be careful what you promise!

I am a woman deeply troubled… I have been pouring out my soul before the Lord… I have been speaking out of my great anxiety and vexation all this time (1 Samuel 1:15–17).

AS

The song of David

The Lord is my rock, my fortress and my deliverer, my God, my rock, in whom I take refuge, my shield and the horn of my salvation, my stronghold and my refuge, my saviour; you save me from violence… He brought me out into a broad place; he delivered me, because he delighted in me.

King David was known as 'Israel's singer of songs' (2 Samuel 23:1 NIV). He wrote most of the psalms, and it was through him that 'songs of deliverance' became an established part of worship in Israel. In fact, the psalms of David have provided inspiration for worship right down to the present day. In these songs we find not only themes of national and personal deliverance, but themes that reflect David's intimate relationship with God, as well as a real sense of the prophetic concerning the nature of the coming Messiah.

Today's reading is the only one of David's psalms to be recorded outside the book of Psalms itself. It is as though the chronicle writer decided that this was the psalm that best reflected David's life and attitude as a whole. It was written after the Lord had delivered David from his enemies, and especially from King Saul, who was passionately jealous of David (1 Samuel 18:9; 19:1) and was determined to kill him. David spent a lot of time on the run from Saul, hiding in caves and sometimes bringing Saul's wrath on those who provided him with food, shelter and weapons. But the Lord did not give David into Saul's hand (1 Samuel 23:14), because he delighted in David.

What is so encouraging about David's song of deliverance is his personal testimony that the Lord can deliver an individual from an enemy that is too mighty for that person to deal with alone. We are not talking about the domestic backbiting that wore Hannah down, but the massed power that a king can bring to bear on an individual.

Read and meditate on today's passage. Pray for those you know who are facing overwhelming situations and need the Lord's hand of deliverance.

AS

The song of Mary

My soul magnifies the Lord, and my spirit rejoices in God my Saviour… His mercy is for those who fear him from generation to generation… He has helped his servant Israel, in remembrance of his mercy, according to the promise he made to our ancestors.

Mary's song of deliverance is amazingly similar to Hannah's song in 1 Samuel 2. It may be worth taking a few minutes to read both songs one after the other and compare them for yourself. Both songs were sung by women; and both were sung in the context of the birth, or imminent birth of a male child that had been marked out by the Lord to further his plans for Israel. Hannah was the mother of Samuel, who ushered in the age of the kings and the prophets, and Mary was the mother of Jesus, the promised Messiah.

When we looked at Hannah's song, we saw that there was a hidden expression of messianic hope, even in a song of personal deliverance. The song was probably known to Mary, and in it she probably recognized an echo of her own situation. From the message the angel had brought her at Jesus' conception, she knew that the messianic part of that song was about to be fulfilled with the birth of her own child. Singing her own version of Hannah's song was a way of telling others that Israel's deliverance was near, that the promised and long-awaited Messiah was at the door (vv. 54–55).

The personal aspect of Mary's song is seen in the way Mary trusts the Lord for personal deliverance; the rescuing of her reputation despite her trying circumstances—she, an unmarried mother, would be remembered for ever as the mother of the Son of God.

Lord God, we leave our reputations in your capable hands; we know we can trust you to deliver us, because you see the greater picture. Help us to trust you to use our difficult circumstances to advance your kingdom on earth, even if we never get to know the whole of it this side of glory. Amen.

AS

The song of Simeon

Simeon took him (Jesus) in his arms and praised God, saying, 'Master, now you are dismissing you servant in peace, according to your word; for my eyes have seen your salvation (deliverance), which you have prepared in the presence of all peoples, a light for revelation to the Gentiles and for glory to your people Israel.'

The song of Simeon is the last song of deliverance in our Bible. It is a short song, almost like the full stop at the end of generations of heartfelt outpouring of messianic hope. Simeon was a devout man and was actively looking for the coming of the Messiah. The Holy Spirit had told him he would not die before he had seen God's promise fulfilled, and so he was watchful (v. 26).

When Simeon sees Jesus being brought to the temple, the Holy Spirit tells him this baby was the Messiah, and he says, 'My eyes have seen your salvation'. For 'salvation' we can just as easily read 'deliverance'. Simeon's song threads together some of the messianic prophecies of Isaiah to show that all the prophetic words in previous songs of deliverance have found their fulfilment here in the person of Jesus (Isaiah 40:5; 49:6; 52:10).

From now on there is no need to sing the same kind of song of deliverance; those who believe in the Messiah get to learn to sing a new song. The new song is one in which the singers know salvation has been attained in Christ; the only record we get of such a song in the New Testament is in Ephesians 5:14: 'Sleeper, awake! Rise from the dead and Christ will shine on you.' This song really does show that Jesus did become a light to the Gentiles.

What do we learn from Simeon? To be led by the Spirit, to listen to the Spirit's prompting, and to be alert and watchful, so that we know where our deliverance is coming from and recognize it when it arrives.

There is salvation in no one else, for there is no other name under heaven… by which we must be saved (Acts 4:12).

AS

Deliverance from sin

Happy are those whose transgression is forgiven, whose sin is covered... I acknowledged my sin to you and I did not hide my iniquity... and you forgave the guilt of my sin... You are a hiding place for me; you preserve me from trouble; you surround me with glad cries of deliverance.

We have spent a week looking at the songs of deliverance sung by people in the Bible. Over the next week, we will be concentrating on aspects of deliverance found in the psalms of David. As we noticed before, David was Israel's singer of songs, and the heartfelt emotion he poured into his songs of deliverance still resonate in our personal experience and are a valuable source of teaching, inspiration and strength.

The one thing from which we need delivering that is common to all of us is sin. There's no avoiding it. None of us match up to what God would have us be, and there is nothing we can do personally to disentangle ourselves from the mess that sin causes in our lives. The essence of the Christian message is that Christ Jesus came into the world to save sinners (1 Timothy 1:15), i.e. to deliver us from sin. He is our Deliverer in that he took the punishment we deserved upon himself, so that if we come to God the Father, acknowledging Jesus' action and asking forgiveness, we can be set free.

Even in the days before Jesus, David knew that God's forgiveness had the power to deliver a sinner from inner bondage. Silence and denial cripples the soul (vv. 3–4), but owning up to our failings before God opens the opportunity to have our guilt taken away (v. 5). The old hymn writers often used to describe sin as a burden, and it is true—to know that your guilt is taken away is like having a heavy load removed from your shoulders. Suddenly the way forward seems easier to face and songs of deliverance well up from the heart.

Steadfast love surrounds those who trust in the Lord. Be glad in the Lord and rejoice... (vv. 10, 11).

AS

Deliverance from fear

I sought the Lord and he answered me, and delivered me from all my fears. Look to him, and be radiant; so your faces shall never be ashamed.

Fear is a disabling and crippling emotion. Fear curtails our potential and prevents us from living life in abundance. We all fear different things, from spiders to terminal illness, and in the world of post-11 September 2001 there have been times when fear in the midst of us has been almost tangible. Fear, like sin and lack of forgiveness, can exert a stranglehold on our lives that we need to be delivered from so that we can live free from its disabling effects.

My main fear revolves around my mother's long-term illness. She suffered from a severe form of arteriosclerosis that began in her early 40s and led to a series of strokes and major paralysis. By 47 she was in a nursing home, where she stayed until she died 15 years later. Having seen the devastating effects of my mother's illness on our family, I am often fearful that the same thing will happen again with me and my family. Perhaps you have similar fears?

I have done everything I can to ensure that I don't follow in my mother's footsteps. However, even when we've done everything *we* can, we find fear has a spiritual dimension that can only be resolved by the Lord. Ultimately it all boils down to trust—trusting the Lord to be with us and strengthen us, whatever life throws at us. Dwelling in his presence puts our fear in perspective; daily surrendering our lives to him rather than grabbing on to what is not ours to keep anyway.

The Lord is the stronghold of my life; of whom [or what] shall I be afraid? … One thing I asked of the Lord, that I will seek after: to live in the house of the Lord all the days of my life [however long it is], to behold the beauty of the Lord [not look inward in self-pity], and to inquire in his temple (Psalm 27:1b, 4).

AS

Deliverance from trouble

When the righteous cry for help, the Lord hears, and rescues them from all their troubles. The Lord is near to the brokenhearted, and saves the crushed in spirit. Many are the afflictions of the righteous, but the Lord rescues them from them all.

We all have to face troubles. Last week the wing mirror was knocked off our new car, my husband lost his mobile phone, we were woken up four nights running by disturbances outside the house and the list goes on… Today's passage tells us that 'many are the afflictions of the righteous', in other words, just because you're a Christian, it doesn't mean that life suddenly becomes a bed of roses; often it is the opposite. The difference should be found in the way we deal with all the hassle.

At the end of a troublesome day I can realize I've got so caught up in the bother that I've forgotten to stop and call out to the Lord for help. Then it helps to lie in bed in the dark and tell the Lord the whole list of troubles. I usually end up asking the Lord for forgiveness for handling things badly, and determining to apologize to various people—if only I'd stopped and asked the Lord to show me the way out at the time!

Some troubles are not trivial, leaving us brokenhearted and crushed in spirit. There is no way round these troubles, only through; yet the Lord is near us in these difficult times; he comforts, guides and strengthens. In every Valley of Achor ('Valley of Trouble or Tears') the Lord has placed an open door, a door of hope—a way out into the promise he has in store for us. It can take time to see the door and reach it, and courage to step through it, but be assured that the Lord is right by you every step of the way.

I will… speak tenderly to her… and (will) make the Valley of Achor a door of hope… there she shall respond as in the days of her youth (Hosea 2:14–15).

AS

Deliverance from distress

He raises up the needy out of distress, and makes their families like flocks. The upright see it and are glad; and all wickedness stops its mouth. Let those who are wise give heed to these things, and consider the steadfast love of the Lord.

I was wondering what the difference was between trouble and distress, as the Lord is credited with delivering us from both. Trouble causes bother and anxiety, but it appears that distress is more acute; causing mental pain and anguish, or it can be trouble caused by financial difficulties. If you ask me, the first could more likely than not be a result of the second!

I never cease to be amazed at the way the Lord delivers us from financial trouble—not that we make a habit of courting such trouble, but sometimes events overtake the best of us! We recently came back from a summer holiday that ended up costing us four times as much in incidentals than we had budgeted. After being scraped up off the floor by my husband, not a little prayer and some creative accounting delivered us from something I thought would distress us until the new year. It was nothing less than a miracle, and our prayer partners were glad!

The Lord may be able to bend the way numbers add up in a most inexplicable way so that a little goes a long way, but we need to do our part too. It is my sincere belief that unless we are honouring the Lord with the way we use our financial assets, we haven't any right to expect him to bail us out when we encounter the unexpected. This doesn't just mean that we should give to the Lord's work, but that we should use what is left for ourselves wisely and prayerfully— then we will witness the steadfast love of the Lord, which David constantly draws out attention to throughout the whole psalm.

Let them thank the Lord for his steadfast love… for he satisfies the thirsty, and the hungry he fills with good things (vv. 8–9).

AS

Deliverance from the wicked

The salvation of the righteous is from the Lord; he is their refuge in the time of trouble. The Lord helps them and rescues them; he rescues them from the wicked and saves them, because they take refuge in him.

Someone approached a member of our church recently and said, 'You go to *that* church, don't you? D'you know what your vicar did?' The mind boggles! 'He lit a bonfire and the smoke went all over our washing!' I was expecting a lot worse, as people can be very wicked with their rumours and accusations. But what shocked me about this one was that the bonfire happened over seven years ago, and we had apologized profusely when our sin was brought to our attention! I was about to get indignant when the Lord reminded me that this was not an attitude I should cultivate in my heart; rather, I should 'refrain from anger… and not fret, as it only leads to evil' (v. 8).

Jesus tells us we are counted among the blessed if people revile us, persecute us and utter evil falsely against us because we make it clear we belong to him (Matthew 5:11). Our reaction should be to bless those who make life difficult for us and to pray constructively for them. The way of Christ is not to repay like with like—a wicked deed with a wicked deed, an unkind word with an unkind word, or a heartfelt grudge with the same or worse. David encourages us to keep to the Lord's way, with the result that 'he will exalt you' (v. 34).

We may not be delivered from 'the wicked' (v. 7), but however long it takes, our job is to leave our reputations in the Lord's hands and serve him by loving those who make life difficult for us (vv. 5 and 6)—practically, as well as in spirit (Romans 12:20).

Pray for people outside the fellowship of your church who have deliberately made life difficult for you. Bless them, forgive them, and ask for opportunities to show them God's love.

                                                              AS

Deliverance from sickness

O Lord my God, I cried to you for help, and you have healed me... You have turned my mourning into dancing; you have taken off my sackcloth and clothed me with joy, so that my soul may praise you and not be silent.

We recently had a service in church where people had an opportunity to share the healing they had received from the Lord. There was one woman who read aloud from the Bible, after which we learnt that six months previously she couldn't speak or eat, and that the doctors were now completely perplexed by her recovery and progress. This woman's whole attitude to life is reflected by the above verses from today's reading—you can see it written all over her—it's wonderful.

Unless you have experienced the nagging feeling of suspecting there is something wrong with you, the visits to the doctor, the long drawn out time waiting for the results of tests, the uncertainty of not knowing, it can be difficult to identify with the sense of mourning that begins within you. Suddenly sunshine and birdsong are more important than clean carpets and a clear sink, touching and togetherness more important than deadlines and committee meetings; there is a real sense of grieving and a possible 'goodbye'. In this situation you can do no more than cry to the Lord for help (v. 2), ask for grace and help (v. 10) and his healing (vv. 8–9).

We *believe* in a God who heals, and never are our prayers more heartfelt and earnest than when we or someone we love is seriously ill (vv. 8–9). And I *know* God heals because I can 'dance' in 3-inch heels on an ankle that once wouldn't bend far enough to let me kneel, but I have no answers to the questions that ask 'Why me?' or 'Why haven't I been made well?' I can only say that whatever happens, I hope God would hear and answer the prayer, 'Be gracious to me, and be my helper.'

O Lord my God, I will give thanks to you for ever (v. 12b).

AS

Deliverance from death

Then I called on the name of the Lord: 'O Lord, I pray save my life!' … For you have delivered my soul from death, my eyes from tears, my feet from stumbling. I walk before the Lord in the land of the living. I kept my faith, even when I said, 'I am greatly afflicted'.

I have never stared death right in the face through illness or accident; though, like most of us, from time to time I have had my nose pushed right up against the window of my own mortality. However, I am sure most of us have been closer to death than we've realized on more than one occasion, saved only by an intervening angel. I still can't figure out how the bottom of a loose stairgate that one of my toddlers lifted up didn't kill my crawling daughter as he let go of it just as she scuttled underneath…

Many people can testify how God has dramatically delivered them from death. But eventually we will all die. The death that we are all delivered from, however, is the 'second death' (Revelation 21:8), reserved for those whose name is not written in the book of life (Revelation 20:13–15). Jesus has promised eternal life to all those that trust in him and follow him (John 3:16), in this way he has become the ultimate Deliverer for all who believe in him.

Today's psalm is just as relevant if we read it with deliverance from the 'second death' in mind as deliverance from death per se. Facing up to our failings and the hopelessness of our situation without a Saviour produces the same set of emotions as being sharply confronted with our own mortality. But God hears us and is merciful (v. 5), and we can live with souls at rest because we are assured of eternal deliverance.

Flesh and blood cannot inherit the kingdom of God… we will all be changed…this perishable body must put on imperishability… The sting of death is sin. But thanks be to God, who gives us the victory through our Lord Jesus Christ (1 Corinthians 15:50ff).

AS

An encouraging letter

We always give thanks to God for all of you and mention you in our prayers, constantly remembering before our God and Father your work of faith and labour of love and steadfastness of hope in our Lord Jesus Christ.

Written in about AD50, only about 20 years after Jesus' death and resurrection, this letter is the earliest of Paul's letters in the New Testament, giving us a fascinating insight into the life of the Church at its beginnings.

Paul had been able to spend only a short time (between three weeks and six months) in Thessalonica, starting and establishing the church there, before he had to leave because of opposition (Acts 17:1–10). He is writing from Athens to find out how the young church is doing and to encourage them to keep going despite continuing persecution. He is also defending himself against false accusations about his motives.

How do you feel when a letter from a friend or relation smiles up at you from among the bills and the junk mail? I love receiving personal letters. They can be particularly helpful when, for example, someone writes, not because they *have* to, like a reply or a request, but because they *want* to. Perhaps they simply want to foster the relationship. Perhaps they know that I have been having a hard time, and want to encourage me, or to help me avoid some pitfall.

Paul's first letter to the Thessalonians is that kind of letter: it is warm and caring. It affirms them, but also addresses an issue where he thinks they misunderstand what God is doing. Paul was a loving Christian friend and pastor to this church and I expect they were greatly helped by his letter.

Is there anyone who would be helped or encouraged by a letter from you today? Someone having a hard time—on their own, for example, or away from home.

MD

It's worth it

Our message of the gospel came to you not in word only,
but also in power and in the Holy Spirit... for in spite of
persecution you received the word with joy inspired by the
Holy Spirit, so that you became an example to all the believers
in Macedonia and in Achaia.

The Thessalonian Christians ran into trouble for their faith almost from day one! They were persecuted right from the beginning for responding to the gospel. But they did not give up. Far from it; they were positively joyful.

There are places in the world today where it is costly to become a Christian. Strong pressure to give up their faith is sometimes put on a new Christian by their family. They may even be rejected or disowned. Sometimes there is physical violence against them. Some Christians have been denied promotion because of their faith. Those of us who have not had to face such persecution do well to be thankful and perhaps turn our gratitude into prayer for those who *are* persecuted.

Jesus, in calling us to follow him, did not promise us an easy or trouble-free life. He warned his disciples that, like him, they would have to suffer at times, and challenged would-be followers to count the cost first. He also called his disciples to costly love and self-denial for his sake.

Why then does anyone follow Jesus at all? I suppose the short answer for many people would be 'Because it's worth it'. Even if we suffer in the short-term, we have heaven to look forward to and the sense of being in a right relationship with God now, with his presence and help to live a worthwhile life. This gives a joy deeper than our circumstances, as the Thessalonians experienced—the joy given by the Holy Spirit.

Ponder why being a Christian is worth it for you, and pray for those
who struggle.

                                                                    MD

Misunderstood

For our appeal does not spring from deceit or impure motives or trickery... As you know and as God is our witness, we never came with words of flattery or with a pretext for greed; nor did we seek praise from mortals, whether from you or from others.

Some years ago, at a planning meeting in our church, two people rebuked me sharply for a question I asked, accusing me of trying to impose my own agenda on the group. But I had had no agenda at all, apart from trying to help the group to clarify its aims over the planned project. I am not prone to emotional collapse, but I dissolved into tears. It was most embarrassing, but being misunderstood can really hurt.

We can probably all think of several occasions when we have been misunderstood, some of which may have hurt us a lot. On at least some of these occasions we were probably partly responsible: perhaps for not expressing things clearly, or at the right time. When misunderstanding occurs, it is good, if we have the opportunity, to explain the truth clearly and calmly, without resentment.

That is what Paul is doing in this passage. He has been accused of ulterior motives in starting the church in Thessalonica and is presumably afraid that some church members may believe the accusation. So he writes to defend himself and explain his true motivation, which is his love and care for them (v. 8). He also points out how hard he worked to provide his own keep, rather than be a burden to them (v. 9).

Something I strongly dislike about some soap operas is the way people jump to hasty conclusions about other people's motives. I know it makes for more exciting programmes, but it sets a very bad example of how to conduct relationships. In real life we need to listen carefully to people before coming to conclusions about them.

Lord, make me careful to understand others and ready to forgive when I am misunderstood.

                                                                      MD

Handling frustration

As for us, brothers and sisters… we longed with great eagerness to see you face to face. For we wanted to come to you—certainly I, Paul, wanted to again and again—but Satan blocked our way.

A few years ago, I believed that God was calling me to serve him in a particular way. I really wanted to do it, but someone else kept blocking my path, for reasons that in my opinion were based on a misunderstanding. I felt very frustrated. The way did eventually open up a few years later and God had used the delay for my growth, but it was still puzzling.

In today's passage we see Paul's very human longing to see the Thessalonian church. However, Paul did not get what he wanted. He was thwarted in his attempts to go and visit his friends. When we find our longings thwarted, we may wonder why. Is Satan getting in the way of something good? Or is God preventing us from fulfilling a desire that was misguided? Sometimes the desire may be good, but the method or the timing wrong. Sometimes the desire itself may not be pleasing to God. We need God's discernment, because the answer to these questions will determine whether we should try to find a way round the obstacle, or to find out what God wants us to hope for instead. There is no ready-made answer.

In our passage, Paul ascribes the obstacle to Satan, obviously believing that his desire to see the Thessalonian church was good and not displeasing to God. He therefore thinks of another way of making contact—no, not by mobile phone! We shall read about it tomorrow.

Father, thank you that it is all right to have human needs and longings. Please work in me by your Spirit, so that I learn both to desire the best and to find your ways forward when I feel frustrated.

MD

Help worth having

*Therefore when we could bear it no longer, we decided to be left
alone in Athens; and we sent Timothy, our brother and co-
worker... to strengthen and encourage you... so that no one
would be shaken by these persecutions. Indeed, you yourselves
know that this is what we are destined for.*

How helpless we feel when someone we care about is going through
a hard time—a difficult relationship, illness, bereavement or anything else. Our instinct is to want to make it all better, but we can't.
What *can* we do that will actually help?

There are several helpful lessons to be drawn from what Paul did
to help the persecuted Thessalonian church. Other people have
helped me in similar ways.

- *He understood* what they were going through. He too had suffered
  persecution (vv. 3–4 and Acts 17). We don't have to have experienced the same as someone else, but they will usually sense if we
  have known suffering.
- *He really cared about them.* They mattered to him and he *longed* to
  know that they were all right (vv. 1, 5).
- *He found a way round the obstacles* that prevented his visit to
  them—he made sure they had someone else, Timothy. This meant
  Paul himself being left on his own (vv. 1–2).
- *He continued his efforts,* by sending them this letter we are study-
  ing. He didn't give up after the failure of his first attempt to get in
  touch. For some of us nowadays writing a letter may require some
  effort. In Paul's day it was a much bigger enterprise.
- *He helped them to think about where God was in the situation,* reminding them the situation was not out of God's control. Paul had
  warned them that being Christians would mean having some persecution (vv. 3–4). Jesus, too, had warned that following him
  would have its cost.

---

*Lord, show me how to give help that is worth having to those who
struggle. Thank you for all those who have helped me when things
were hard.*

MD

Warming the pastor's heart

Timothy has just now come to us from you, and has brought us the good news of your faith and love… For this reason, brothers and sisters, during all our distress and persecution we have been encouraged about you through your faith. For we now live, if you continue to stand firm in the Lord.

I remember the first time I managed to grow tomatoes from seed. After the first flush of enthusiasm, I found it quite an effort to keep watering them and pinching out side shoots. But eventually I discovered the joy that comes from nurturing something into life and fruitful growth.

On a much more important level there is the joy, which Paul describes in this passage, of seeing your costly efforts bearing fruit in the lives of other people. I was surprised in my preparation for today's notes, when I read how Paul expresses his reaction to the news of the Thessalonians' continuing faith and love. He not only speaks of his joy and encouragement, but he says, 'we now live'.

And if human pastors can be so warmed and animated by seeing the growth of spiritual life and love in those they care for, how much more delighted must God himself be when he sees these things in us. I am reminded of Jesus' story of the lost sheep in Luke 15. He says there is more joy in heaven over one sinner who repents than over 99 righteous people who do not need to repent. And I should think the joy level over the latter would be pretty high!

To know that we might give God joy can be an incentive to us to keep going (and growing!) in our Christian life.

If you recognize that you have a pastor's heart like Paul's, have you found out how God wants you to use it to care for his people? It will probably bring you some heartache, but also great joy.

MD

Great expectations

Now may our God and Father himself and our Lord Jesus Christ direct our way to you. And may the Lord make you increase and abound in love for one another and for all just as we abound in love for you. And may he so strengthen your hearts in holiness that you may be blameless.

Have you ever heard anyone pray a prayer that you think may be asking God for too much? Many years ago, I was leading a small group's study on the promise 'If two of you agree on earth about anything you ask, it will be done' (Matthew 18:19). I suggested that we should put our study into practice by praying for something we all agreed on, and see the next week what had happened. Someone suggested praying for the release of a deaf teenager who had been held by terrorists for several weeks already. Help! This was really nailing our colours to the mast. But everyone agreed, so we did it. I must admit I felt a little worried on God's behalf! Imagine my delight (and some surprise, I confess) when the teenager was freed a few days later.

In today's passage, Paul is asking for three big things:

- *First*, he prays that God will enable him to visit the Thessalonian church. In view of previous obstacles, this may be difficult, but not impossible.
- *Next*, he prays that the Lord will make their love grow, not only for one another, but also for everyone. It is hard enough to show consistent, unselfish love for a few people, never mind for all! What a big prayer!
- *Third*, Paul prays for them to become holy and blameless. This one is enormous.

And yet, surely Paul was not wrong to pray these prayers, because at least the last two are certainly God's will. God wants the highest and best for us all and Paul is entering into God's prayer, praying according to what God wants.

Lord, sometimes my view of you is too small. Please teach me to know you better and trust you more, and to expect great things of you.

MD

Attractive holiness

For this is the will of God, your sanctification: that you abstain from fornication; that each one of you know how to control your own body in holiness and honour, not with lustful passion... For God did not call us to impurity, but in holiness.

What does the word 'holiness', or a 'holy' person conjure up in your mind? For some it is a priggish, kill-joy image. For me, it is a picture of someone with warm, twinkling eyes, full of fun and deep love, a person totally available for God. The 'feel' is of real freedom, because such a person would be free from the dictates of their self-ish desires: free to be and to do what pleases God. They would also presumably be good at hearing what God says. If I met such a person, they would be able to show me more of God and help me to hear what God is saying.

I find this a very attractive picture and I want to be like that. Verse 3 tells me that God wants me to be like that too: 'sanctification', which means 'being made holy', is God's will for us all. This is not an instant transformation but a process, and it requires our co-operation—the obedience bit. Paul talks here about doing what God wants in sexual matters: not wronging or exploiting others by having sex outside marriage (v. 6). Of course obeying God is important in all other areas of life, too, and Paul deals with some of these elsewhere. Doing what God wants when we have a strong urge to do something else can be very difficult, but we have the Holy Spirit to help us. The issue is whether we really want help and will pray for it.

If we do, as well as praying 'Please help me', we might pray, 'Lord, I want to be holy', or 'Lord, I want to be all yours', to remind us of the holiness we are aiming at: the image of twinkling eyes, love and freedom.

MD

Too heavenly minded?

But we urge you, beloved, to (love one another) more and more, to aspire to live quietly, to mind your own affairs, and to work with your hands, as we directed you, so that you may behave properly toward outsiders and be dependent on no one.

The nights of the year when many children find it hardest to go to sleep are the nights before something big is going to happen— something exciting, like Christmas, their birthday, or going off on holiday, perhaps. Or something about which they are anxious, maybe starting school, or going into hospital. They, and adults too at times, are restless and find it hard to be relaxed or still enough to drop off to sleep.

Some members of the Thessalonian church were in this situation, believing as they did that Christ was about to return to earth at any moment to usher in the end of the age. Some of them were not doing any work and, therefore, sponging on others presumably. They were restless themselves and unsettled other people. Paul urges them to 'aspire to live quietly'. This might mean earnestly asking God for his peace, which is a good thing for us all to do in times of stress or uncertainty. Or Paul might be telling Christians not to spend our time seeking exciting 'spiritual experiences'. God may give us these, but our priority is to concentrate on the normal spiritual disciplines—such as prayer, reading the Bible and learning to love God and other people.

We also do well to work hard at our responsibilities, bearing burdens for others more than being a burden to them, though of course we must receive gladly and graciously too. I was once very sad to hear someone say of a fellow Christian, 'She is a "taker" in life, rather than a "giver".'

Loving Father, please help me not to be so heavenly minded that I am no earthly use. And, by your Spirit, make me a 'giver' rather than a 'taker'.

MD

Rest in peace

But we do not want you to be uninformed, brothers and sisters, about those who have died, so that you may not grieve as others do who have no hope... For this we declare to you by the word of the Lord, that we who are alive, who are left until the coming of the Lord, will by no means precede those who have died.

Some of the Thessalonians were anxious about something that may seem rather strange to us. This was only about 20 years after the resurrection and theirs was still a young church, so they had not known the death of many fellow Christians. Also, they were expecting Jesus to return at any moment to bring about the end of this world and usher in the kingdom of God. The worrying question for them was whether Christians who died before Jesus' return would miss out on heaven.

Paul reassures them that those who have died 'in Christ' will not miss out: they will rise first to meet the Lord and those who are alive will then join them, and all Christians will be with the Lord together for ever. This reassurance comes on the basis of 'the word of the Lord', by which Paul presumably means that God said it particularly clearly to him. It fits, also, with God's character: he loves and makes provision for all those who respond to him, not merely some.

From our perspective, almost 2,000 years later, the worry seems unnecessary—so many Christians have died, including all the apostles and many saintly people, that we presume they will all get to heaven. But we may have different worries or questions about death. All the answers depend on the goodness and love of God, and as we come to understand the Bible better we shall probably find some of these answers.

Paul tells us that all Christians will one day be together with Christ. How might this truth help us when a Christian loved one dies?

MD

Be prepared!

For you yourselves know very well that the day of the Lord will come like a thief in the night... So then let us not fall asleep as others do, but let us keep awake and be sober.

Each of the four times that I realized I was pregnant, the thought occurred to me, 'However and whenever it happens, one day there will be an end to this pregnancy.' And each time, towards the end of the nine months, I followed the advice to have my case packed a couple of weeks before the baby was due, ready for a speedy dash to hospital when the time came. The advice was good, as each child arrived before the due date.

Paul says that the second coming (the return of Jesus Christ on the 'day of the Lord') is like pregnancy in that the labour pains will certainly come sometime, even if the exact date is not known. (There were no planned Caesarean sections before the onset of natural labour in those days!) Jesus' earthly life and his second coming are inextricably bound together as part of God's work of saving the world. Paul says also that the second coming is like the coming of a thief in the night, in that it is unexpected and sudden.

Paul, therefore, exhorts Christians to be prepared for it at any time. That means being ready all the time. But how? Paul's words, 'Keep awake and be sober' are obviously not about sleep patterns and alcohol! He means attending to:

- *Alertness*—living our whole lives with an eye on Jesus' return.
- *Faith*—learning to trust God more. (He doesn't want us to be anxious or afraid.)
- *Love*—growing in love for God and other people.
- *Hope*—looking forward to the life of heaven that Jesus will bring.

Lord, please show me how to build these things into my daily life, in order to be ready for your coming, but without becoming stressed or anxious about them.

MD

Harmonious relationships

Be at peace among yourselves… See that none of you repays evil for evil, but always seek to do good to one another and to all.

When they lived at home, our children had their conflicts like many others, but with all our children having left home now, one thing that gives Graham and me great joy is to see them loving and caring for each other. They keep in touch with each other by phone and e-mail and visit each other from time to time. They enter into each other's joys and sorrows, and care and pray if one has a problem.

When I first noticed how much pleasure all this gave to me, it also dawned on me that it might be something like God's pleasure when his people love and care for one another. I know families where the children's antagonism towards each other brings pain and grief to their parents. I wonder whether this grief gives us an inkling of how God grieves over unloving relationships, especially within the Church. Is it not only Paul, but God too, who longs for the Christians at Thessalonica to be at peace among themselves?

And what about *our* churches? How can we delight God by being at peace among ourselves? Paul says, 'Do not repay evil for evil'. We all receive emotional knocks from other people from time to time, but we need to forgive and let go of the hurts, so that we can move forward in freedom. If we don't do this, we may well suffer more than the 'offender'. And God will be grieved. If we find it hard, it may help us to remember how much God forgives us and that he accepts us, warts and all.

Paul also says we should positively do good to all. Some of his examples are to 'encourage the faint-hearted, help the weak, be patient with all of them'.

If all this sounds too daunting, how about trying to perform a few extra acts of love each day?

MD

Three impossible things
before breakfast?

Rejoice always, pray without ceasing, give thanks in all circumstances; for this is the will of God in Christ Jesus for you.

This may look more like three impossible things all the time! However, when we look more closely at each in turn, they may seem at least possible, even if not always easy.

Rejoice always This is not a command to be happy all the time. Sometimes sad things happen and it is entirely appropriate to feel sad at such times. It is, rather, an exhortation to set our hearts always to be glad about what is good, without denying any sadness in our present situation. For example, we can always remind ourselves that God loves us and is with us, and we can set ourselves to be glad about that, even in the middle of pain and grief.

Pray without ceasing It may be that this is partly about not giving up on prayer, but there is more to it than that. We obviously cannot give our whole attention to prayer all the time. Our minds must attend to other things too, some of which require great concentration. However, just as being with another person can include being in their company without necessarily attending to them directly, so with God. Praying without ceasing includes simple, sensitive awareness of God's presence—doing everything in God's company.

Give thanks in all circumstances This is not telling us to give thanks *for* all circumstances, some of which may not be good, but *in* all circumstances. In Romans 8:28, Paul tells us that in all things God works for good for those who love him. That means that however bad things may be, God will bring good out of them for us. So we can always thank God for the good he will bring, even when we are not grateful for what is happening. Thanksgiving is very good for us spiritually, as it really strengthens our faith.

How could you begin to establish these habits, probably one at a time?
                                                                    MD

Goodbye / Into God's keeping

May the God of peace himself sanctify you entirely; and may your spirit and soul and body be kept sound and blameless at the coming of our Lord Jesus Christ. The one who calls you is faithful and he will do this.

'Goodbye' is a word we use so often, but rarely think about what it really means. It is a contraction of 'God be with you (ye)', and implies the desire that God will be constantly protecting and taking care of someone while we are no longer with them. Having forgotten the derivation of 'goodbye', we have also lost its prayerful meaning. Instead, at the end of a letter to someone we love, or when saying goodbye to them, we often say things like, 'I hope such and such goes well', or 'Have a safe journey'. There is nothing wrong with these good wishes, but would it encourage people more if we also said something like, 'and may God be with you'?

Paul is writing in Greek and did not of, course, know English, but the ending of his letter has the same 'feel' as the original meaning of 'goodbye'. What he most wants for his beloved Thessalonian church members is for God to be with them, to make them more and more like Jesus and to take them safely through this life to heaven.

He not only tells them of his longings for them, but also of his confidence that God will do these things for them. When confidence seems to be based merely on optimism, or wishful thinking, it can be irritating, because it doesn't offer us a way of becoming confident too. Here, however, Paul's confidence *can* be shared, because it is based on the faithfulness of God. God, the God of peace, is trustworthy: he has promised always to be with his people and he always keeps his word.

Goodbye. And may the grace of our Lord Jesus Christ be with you— today and always.

MD

A long, long time ago...

Where are your forefathers now?

Zechariah is a book which few people can find in a hurry. (See how long it takes *you!*) It is tucked away near the very end of the Old Testament. Obviously, a lot of Israelite history has flowed under the bridge by the time Zechariah appears on the scene. But Zechariah is crucial to the history of Israel. In order to best appreciate why, it's worth a quick overview of what's gone before.

About 1280BC Moses leads the people of Israel out of Egypt. In the wilderness Yahweh (Jehovah) makes a covenant with them. He has chosen them to be his people, and they gratefully accept him as their God. But this special relationship carries special obligations: the people must obey Yahweh's laws. Yahweh then leads the people through the wilderness to the edge of the 'promised land'.

By 1200BC Jericho has fallen, and the Israelite conquest of Canaan, their 'promised land', has begun. About 1000BC David is crowned king of Israel, and then Solomon builds the great temple in Jerusalem. It's Israel's 'golden age', but the people are not faithful to Yahweh. Kings, good and bad, come and go, until in about 931BC, Israel finally splits into two kingdoms, with two kings: the northern kingdom, Israel, under Jeroboam I, and the southern kingdom, Judah, under Rehoboam.

Then it's downhill all the way for the ten tribes that make up the northern kingdom. They worship other gods until judgment falls. In 722BC the Assyrians invade the northern kingdom, and carry the people off to slavery in Assyria. These Israelites dwindle away into nothing.

Israel's 'time-line' with God fills the Old Testament. What about *your* time-line with God? Have you ever made one out, charting in the date when *your* 'covenant' with him (in Christ) began, and all the highs and lows since?

Today's study ends on a low note: Do you know Christians who have constantly put other things before God for so long that finally their faith, too, is conquered and dwindles away into nothing?

Read 2 Kings 17.

AC

You wouldn't listen

*The Lord Almighty has done to us what our ways
and practices deserve.*

After the fall of the northern kingdom in 722BC, the Bible turns its attention to the remaining two tribes of Israel, which made up the little kingdom of Judah. Sadly, these people had learned nothing from the Assyrian disaster that overtook their fellow Israelites. They also abandon the covenant with Yahweh.

Over the years Yahweh sends a succession of messengers, or prophets, to warn this remaining part of Israel of their great danger, to call them to repentance. Yahweh wants the people to stop worshipping bits of wood, and to stop committing gross deeds. He wants them to return to a fruitful and loving relationship with him, and to treat each other with justice.

Thus we come to the great eighth-century prophets, Isaiah and Jeremiah. Read them, and you'd think their messages of God's heartbroken love would melt a heart of stone. But not Israel's! So finally, in 587BC, God's judgment falls on the southern kingdom. The Babylonians invade, rampage through Jerusalem, and do the unthinkable—they destroy the temple. For the people of Israel, this is the end of the world. The Babylonians laugh at their captives' horror, and carry them off into exile. (Hence the ancient song: 'By the waters of Babylon I sat down and wept...') No wonder the Israelites wept: everything had been taken from them. Too late they remembered that their beloved land and freedom depended on their faithfulness to the covenant with Yahweh.

The exile lasted about 70 years. During this time, God sent Israel the prophet Ezekiel. He wanted them back into the covenant relationship. But until they obeyed, he could do nothing with them.

If you've ever done something really wrong, that's landed you in well-deserved trouble, you'll know all about exile. It's a lonely place, full of bitter regrets. Damage done to other people can take years to heal. Begin today by turning to God. Repentance has always been the first step back from exile.

Read 2 Chronicles 36:11–21 and Ezekiel 11:16–25.

AC

Home-coming

*Lord… you have been angry… these seventy years… Come,
O Zion! Escape, you who live in the Daughter of Babylon! …
The Lord… will again choose Jerusalem… The hands of
Zerubbabel have laid the foundation of this temple.*

539BC, and the ancient near east was in turmoil. Cyrus, King of Persia, had overthrown the vast Babylonian empire. Suddenly the Israelite exiles were under Persian rule. Persian rule was liberal, for Cyrus let captive peoples return to their homelands. So—against all hope—little Israel was not just allowed, but encouraged to go back to Jerusalem! In 538BC, Zerubbabel, grandson of Israelite King Jehoiachin, led about 50,000 exiled Israelites home. Jerusalem was in ruins and the temple a heap of stones. Nevertheless, this was a major watershed in Israelite history—the exile was over. Yahweh had again rescued his people.

Ezra tells the story in a most moving way. He stresses that all the restoration work was done 'according to the instructions written in the Law of Moses'. Everything was now to be done *properly*. Israel had learned their lesson in ignoring Yahweh's laws. This time they were going to follow them to the letter. Israel had 'come home' in more ways than one.

Restoring the temple at this time was absolutely vital to Israel's survival. The temple was the major, visible sign that Israel was back in daily business with God. The temple restored would proclaim a people forgiven and restored to their covenant with Yahweh. And yet—various new 'settlers' in Jerusalem so opposed the rebuilding that gradually the Israelites became discouraged. Building work finally ground to a dismal halt. Here things rested, in rubble, for 18 years.

The returned exiles were back from exile, but not moving forward. They were in grave danger. They risked losing their vision of what they were all about. Yahweh's response? To encourage them. He sent Zechariah.

If you've ever tried to build a life that radiates your inner commitment to God, you'll know about dismal side-trackings. Who has God sent to encourage you at such times?

    Read Ezra 1, 3 and 4.

AC

Get moving!

And in the eighth month of the second year of Darius, the word of the Lord came to the prophet Zechariah.

520BC. Darius has replaced Cyrus as King of Persia. The Israelites have lived among the ruins of Jerusalem for 18 years. The temple is still unfinished. And that October or November, the word of the Lord came to the prophet Zechariah…

God called two prophets to speak to his people that year—Haggai and Zechariah. Their books, together with Malachi, tell how Israel did eventually rebuild Jerusalem and the temple. With them, the Old Testament draws to a close: the stage is now set for the coming of Christ (about 400 years later).

So Zechariah played a vital part in Israelite history. At a time when the people had lost their vision, he helped wake Israel up. He kick-started them back into action. And it all began with a call back to the covenant. The prophecies began with: 'Return to me,' declares the Lord Almighty, 'and I will return to you' (1:3). For, through Zechariah, the Lord assures the people that he still loves them: 'I will return to Jerusalem with mercy, and there my house will be rebuilt' (1:16).

He comforts the discouraged priests: 'See, I have taken away your sin, and I will put rich garments on you' (3:4). He reassures the worn-out leader, Zerubbabel, that it will come about 'Not by might nor by power, but by my Spirit,' says the Lord. 'Who despises the day of small things?' demands Zechariah, as the people survey their pitiful attempts at temple restorations. Don't despise the little you have done when you compare it with the task ahead of you, he says in effect. *Just keep going!* And so, under Zechariah, the restoration begins again.

When God calls you to do something, don't let discouragement defeat you. Remember Deuteronomy 31:8: 'The Lord himself goes before you and will be with you; he will never leave you nor forsake you. Do not be afraid; do not be discouraged.'

AC

Unexpected kindness

*Those who are far away will come and help to build the temple of
the Lord, and you will know that the Lord Almighty has sent me
to you.*

Yet when the Israelites resumed their temple restoration, their enemies
immediately attacked. Things looked bad, for this time the 'settlers'
appeal to Darius to stop the Israelites once and for all. But first Darius
decides to check the court records. He discovers a scroll on which
Cyrus had written a decree concerning Israel's return from Babylon.
They were to be given every *assistance* in rebuilding their temple! So
Darius does not stop the Israelites. Instead, he gives official backing—
and, incredibly, goes on to *pay* for the restoration of the temple! Israel's
enemies are mortified.

The Israelites are triumphant. They rejoice in Yahweh's care for
them, and with Zechariah's encouragement, carry on with the work.
In four short years—by 516BC—the temple is well and truly finished.
That year the people are able to celebrate Passover with a fully func-
tioning temple. With the amazing release from Babylon still a 'second
exodus' in living memory, this was a very moving time for the people.

The story is found in the book of Ezra, who adds something that
has great repercussions in the future. In 6:21, he relates how the
Israelites welcomed 'all who had separated themselves from the
unclean practices… in order to seek the Lord'. This was Israel as they
were meant to be: in obedient covenant relationship with Yahweh,
and by joyous example, bringing others into this same covenant relationship with him. Israel was always called to be separate but never
exclusive. Through them God meant to bless *all* the nations of the
world.

When the New Testament Gospel writers tell the story of Jesus' last
days, which reveal him as indeed the Messiah, they quote Zechariah
more than any other prophet. (Read Zechariah 9:9; 12:10; 13:7.)

Some Christians radiate a warm spirituality that attracts other
people to Christ. They, too, live in a close 'covenant relationship' with
God. No relationship with God, no power.

Read Ezra 5 and 6.

AC

Zechariah in his place

During the night I had a vision...

Zechariah lies among the last of the four main sections of the Old Testament. After the Pentateuch, the history books and the Wisdom literature come 17 prophetic books, of which Zechariah is one.

Seventeen books of prophecy! That's a vast amount of prophetic writing. One thing's clear—then, as now, God wanted to communicate with his people. So he sent messengers, or 'prophets'. Thus in the ninth century BC there were Elijah and Elisha (no books remain). In the eighth century along came Jonah, Amos, Hosea, Isaiah and Micah. The seventh century saw Nahum, Habakkuk and Zephaniah. The seventh/sixth centuries held Jeremiah. Then, soon after 587BC and Israel's exile to Babylon, God sent along Obadiah. During the sixth-century exile there was Ezekiel, and, post-exile, Haggai. Along with him came Zechariah. After him, fifth to fourth century BC, was Malachi. (Joel's dates are uncertain.)

Zechariah's prophecies run to 14 chapters. Chapters 1—8 deal with the same time as Haggai. Chapters 9—14 differ in content and language, and 'feel' of a later date, probably fifth century. Whatever the timescale, all of Zechariah is concerned with the same subjects: judgment and salvation for little Judah and the nations; the rebuilding of the temple as a sign of God's presence; and Israel's leaders in relation to God. The coming of the Messiah is foreseen: he will be a priest, governor, branch, humble king and afflicted shepherd.

Today Zechariah still speaks to us—for the *subjects* that concerned him concern us:
- Judgment and salvation? We too will live in guilt and unease until we find forgiveness in Christ.
- Building temples? The New Testament tells us that now our very *bodies* are temples of the Holy Spirit.
- Our leaders? Their morality—or lack of it—still has wide repercussions. Listen to Radio 4 some morning!
- Messiah? Zechariah dared to dream of him; we have the joy of *knowing* him.

Read 1 Corinthians 3:16 and Colossians 1:3–20.

AC

A call from God

On the twenty-fourth day of the eleventh month, the month of Shebat, in the second year of Darius, the word of the Lord came to… Zechariah son of Berekiah, the son of Iddo.

How do you become a prophet? From a perusal of the Old Testament one thing is clear: the 'true' prophets did not choose prophecy as a career move. *God called them*—in an intensely personal, unmistakable way, to be his messengers. His call did not depend on an ability to speak in public. In fact, many prophets were at first overwhelmed with feelings of unworthiness and downright terror. There was just one factor necessary: a heart open towards God, a person already walking in the covenant relationship with Yahweh. God could bless and use such people to bear his message to Israel.

Zechariah was such a man. We don't know much about him personally, other than that when the book opens he is most probably a young man, from a family of priests (1:1, 7). His grandfather, Iddo, had returned from Babylon with the other exiles less than 20 years before.

Zechariah, like all true Old Testament prophets, was given a specific message from God—or series of messages. These encouraged the people in their time of suffering; offered forgiveness; and a chance to renew the covenant promises. The messages came by voice, in visions, and in dreams. They were quite dramatic and unforgettable. Their vividness astonished Zechariah. 'Then I looked up—and there before me were four horns! … a man with a measuring line! … a flying scroll… four chariots…! (Zechariah 1:18; 2:1; 5:1; 6:1).

There was no question of Zechariah keeping such amazing things to himself: he felt compelled to prophesy loud and long!

God still works through people today, and the requirements are the same: a heart for God, and a willingness to obey his call, whatever that might be for you. Zechariah could name the exact day of his calling from God. How specific can *you* be?

Read Jeremiah 1:1–10 and Ezekiel 1:1; 2:1–8.

AC

The visions

During the night I had a vision... a man riding a red horse! ... four horns! ... a man with a measuring line in his hand!

When God gave Zechariah visions, he was speaking in picture language to the Israelites of the fifth century BC. He wanted to tell them their own story from a totally different perspective—a divine one: his own.

Zechariah's first vision, dated 15 February 519 (Zechariah 1:7), sets the stage for all that is to come by summing up 'the story so far...' It begins way out in the spiritual realm, where four horsemen are patrolling the world on God's behalf. Then an angel enquires as to the fate of little Israel. 'How long will you withhold mercy from Jerusalem...?' The Israelites must have wondered that many a time while they sat in Babylon. Now came the answer: the 70 years of the exile were over, and 'the Lord will again comfort Zion' (1:17).

Vision two (1:18–21) yields more spiritual insight into events. The number 'four' speaks of completeness, and cattle 'horns' in ancient times spoke of ruthless power. (And Babylon had indeed so nearly destroyed Israel.) However, God had sent his servants to destroy the 'horns'. (And so Babylon fell to Persia.)

Vision three (2:1–5) is full of hope and new beginnings: the Lord sends a man to measure up the city for rebuilding, and promises that he will be a protecting wall around Jerusalem, a 'glorious presence', for 'whoever touches you touches the apple of his eye' (2:8).

To the discouraged Israelites so recently back from exile, living hand to mouth in the ruins of Jerusalem, Zechariah's words must have shone like warm sunshine upon them. 'Shout and be glad, O Daughter of Zion, for I am coming, and I will live among you' (2:10).

These promises stand true for Christians today. We may make mistakes and end up in dead ends. We can feel dominated and oppressed by people or events. And God often deals with us as he dealt with the Israelites of the fifth century BC: by sending us words of encouragement via other Christians.

Read Philippians 2:1–4.

AC

Let him do it

Then he showed me Joshua the high priest... and Satan
standing at his right side to accuse him... Now Joshua
was dressed in filthy clothes.

It is hard to appreciate the shattering impact these words would have had. The Israelites relied on the high priest to go to God on their behalf. If he was unworthy, then what would become of them? But the vision goes on to reveal that God did not leave Joshua in his shame. Instead, an 'angel of the Lord' gives Joshua clean clothes: 'See, I have taken away your sin, and I will put rich garments on you' (3:4). And in faith Zechariah sees far into the future: that in truth, holiness before God never really depended on the high priest and his fellow priests, anyway. They themselves were only 'men symbolic of things to come'. One day the 'Branch'—Jesus, the ultimate high priest—would come, and 'remove the sin of this land in a single day'.

Years ago a nun in Uganda was discouraged. For years she had denied herself and served other people. Her good works were appreciated, but she had no joy in her faith. She watched enviously the joy of a certain Bishop Festo Kivengere of Kigezi diocese. One day she finally asked him why he was so happy in his faith, and she was not. His answer was simple: 'O Sister, it is because I am rejoicing in what Christ has done for me; not in what I have done for Christ.' The nun stood stunned—and then grinned. 'Yes!' she said. '*Now I understand!*'

Do you ever try—and fail—to be a good Christian? Well, ask yourself what you have *ever* achieved spiritually through your own efforts. Not salvation: Christ died for you, and the Holy Spirit was the one who quickened your spirit to comprehend this and accept it for yourself. So why should you expect to be able to lead a 'good Christian life' by simply trying?

As Zerubbabel found, it is 'not by might nor by power, but by my Spirit,' says the Lord (Zechariah 4:6).

AC

Pictures talk

Then the angel who talked with me returned and wakened me…
'What do you see?'

Gold lampstands, olive trees, flying scrolls, outsize baskets, horse-drawn chariots… such pictures from chapters 4—6 of Zechariah may seem bizarre to us today. Yet these visions certainly helped Israel get a better spiritual perspective on themselves as the temple restoration went on.

So what about the lampstand? Scholars explain that it symbolized the temple and faithful Jewish worshippers. Like a city set on a hill, their light shone out before God and the nations and 'cannot be hid' (Matthew 5:14). So Zerubbabel, in rebuilding this temple, was doing a vital thing. As Zechariah says: 'Who despises the day of small things?' (4:10). The Lord promised Zerubbabel that 'his hands will also *complete* it' (4:9). He was not to be discouraged. There have been many humble Christians whose witness has shone far beyond what they would ever have imagined. Even small lights on a hill can be seen for miles.

What about the olive trees? Scholars say these are two men chosen by God—at this time in Israel the roles of priest and prince (king) supported each other. Later, Jesus would in his single person fulfil both roles of priest and king.

Flying scrolls speak of God's law. The vision reminds Israel that God's word carries power. Evil is punished. And taken far away—as shown in the vision of the woman trapped in a large basket. Here God's angel ensures that no evil can escape to do further damage. It is all carried off on strong wings, far away to the east: at last the cleansing of Israel is complete.

Four horse-drawn chariots? Zechariah's last vision recalls the first, as now God's patrols encompass the earth. The nations have been judged and there will be peace.

In chapter 6 the visions end and we have a poem about a crown for Joshua. A high priest given a king's crown? Puzzling for the Israelites, not for us, it anticipates just one thing—the coming of Jesus, our high priest and king.

Read Hebrews 8 and 9.

AC

Image is not enough

Administer true justice; show mercy and compassion to one another. Do not oppress the widow or the fatherless, the alien or the poor. In your hearts do not think evil of each other.

Some years ago I attended a Presbyterian church in New York State where the six men who took up the collection not only wore identical suits and ties and shirts—but even the *exact same shoes and socks*. They were adamant that their church should 'do things properly'. Likewise, I've been in Anglo-Catholic churches in England where the choreography would not have shamed a theatrical production in the West End. But what lies behind it all? Do matching suits and colourful processions *prove* true godliness is present? I was reminded of these church services when I read chapter 7 of Zechariah.

The date is 7 December 518 (see 7:1!), and some men have arrived at the temple enquiring about the precise details of keeping fasts. And the obvious suddenly dawned on me: the book of Zechariah talks a lot about Israel turning from God, but throughout all their rebellion, Israel never stinted on their elaborate ceremonies that were meant to 'worship' Yahweh. So Zechariah replies by challenging their *motives*. When they fasted in the past, was it for God or for show? During those fasts, the Lord accuses them: 'they refused to pay attention; stubbornly they turned their backs... they made their hearts hard as flint... when I called, they did not listen' (7:11, 12, 13). All that pomp and ceremony *while* they were breaking their covenant with Yahweh. Such a pointless waste of effort! For Yahweh wanted their hearts, not their performances. Just as he still does today.

Chapter 8 goes on to paint a marvellous, heartwarming vision of what Yahweh wanted to provide for Israel. A Jerusalem so safe that old people sit in the sun and children play in the streets. In his great love, Yahweh yearned to bless his people. And if only they responded from the heart, then the sad fasts will be transformed into 'glad occasions and happy festivals'!

Read Isaiah 1:10–20.

AC

Sorting things out

Surely I will redeem them...

God's relationship with Israel sometimes reminds me of my relationship with my over-bold rough collie puppy. Israel constantly refused to listen to God until he withdrew his protection from them—and they suffered for it. My Archie approaches aggressive dogs, heedless of my cries to 'Come, come back!' In exasperation and helplessness I have had to watch him going headlong into German Shepherd or Jack Russell-shaped trouble, part of me thinking: 'Well, this will teach him!'

When indeed he does get snapped at and is in distress, am I glad? No! My love for him overrides everything, and I charge in to defend him against the other dog, who, after all, never starts it in the first place. Archie does, by all his snoopy sniffs.

With chapter 9 of Zechariah, God is having a go at the 'big dogs' who've picked on foolish, heedless little Israel. They include Damascus, Tyre and Sidon, Ashkelon, Gaza, Ekron, and Ashdod. 'I will take the blood from... between their teeth' (9:7), vows the Lord. 'Never again will an oppressor overrun my people, for now I am keeping watch' (9:8). As I wipe the dirt and leaves off Archie, and soothe his whimpers, I know how God feels!

With chapter 9, we have entered the 'second half' of Zechariah, and look to the far future. You may not think you know Zechariah, but you'll be familiar with this from Easter readings: 'See, your king comes to you... gentle and riding on a donkey... He will proclaim peace to the nations' (9:9, 10).

Chapter 10 is brimming with more love. 'Ask the Lord for rain in the springtime', it urges, contrasting his constant care with the total indifference of the pagan gods. I visited a Hindu temple for the first time while in South Africa a few months ago, and the gulf between these gods and the Christian God just staggered me. A Hindu convert to Christianity told me he can never understand how the Israelites could prefer lumps of inert wood to Yahweh. He's been there, done that, and prefers Jesus every time!

Read Zechariah 10.

AC

Look at me

They will look on me...

There are two types of people in this world. The first likes to make a surprise, and spring it on you without any warning. The other kind of person gets so excited themselves, that they can't help dropping hints as to the wonderful thing they are going to give you. I think Yahweh is the second kind of 'person', because throughout the Old Testament he can't help telling the Israelites about Jesus. He doesn't name him, but every time the subject of the future comes up, Yahweh can't quite keep the good news of the coming incarnation to himself.

Yahweh's at it again in chapters 12 and 13: 'And I will pour out on the house of David and the inhabitants of Jerusalem a spirit of grace and supplication. They will look on *me*' (notice he doesn't say 'him'), 'the one they have pierced, and they will mourn' (12:10). When St John, centuries later, came to write his Gospel, he remembered this passage in Zechariah, and referred to it in the crucifixion scene of John 19:34–37.

The Old Testament is the story of Yahweh's covenant with Israel, but with his incarnation and death, all will change. The New Testament is the beginning of the story of God's new covenant with humankind, based on what Jesus has done.

Zechariah describes what happens after the promised One is pierced and dies (chapter 13): 'On that day a fountain will be opened to the house of David and the inhabitants of Jerusalem, to cleanse them from sin and impurity' (v. 1).

But cleansing is just the first step. It is made clear in the New Testament that God's long-term aim for us is to transform us into the likeness of Christ. This is not always a pleasant experience for us! Indeed, such a radical transformation is compared in Zechariah 13 to being thrust into the fire, where Yahweh 'will refine them like silver and test them like gold. They will call on my name and I will answer them; I will say, "They are my people," and they will say, "The Lord is our God".'

Read Galatians 5:16–26.

AC

The last battle

Then the Lord will go out and fight against those nations…

The book of Zechariah covers an enormous time-span. It begins by looking back to the exile in Babylon in 587BC. It ends—with the end of the world! Read chapter 14 and then read Revelation 21 and 22, which echo many of the details found here in this little book tucked away near the end of the Old Testament. It doesn't make for comfortable reading: the events foretold are cataclysmic and violent. Nations will be in convulsions; people will be starving and suffering plague-like diseases. I, for one, hope I'm not around for this final showdown!

Yet there are several points worth noting. The point of the terrible battles is to settle scores: the evildoers pay for the wrong they have done. If this chapter seems terrible to read, just open your daily newspaper and see the horrors that happen daily in this world, every day. All that will be put right. The battles don't go on for ever, and they are not mindless chaos. The Lord is in charge, and when the dust finally settles, good will come out of it. The evil that humanity has brought into the world will be dealt with for ever. In that new day, the love of Yahweh will enhance every aspect of life, however humble.

- You could write your *own* version of Zechariah. Begin with your own rescue from exile in Babylon—the date of your conversion.
- Think back to your early Christian walk, when you first learned you were a temple of the living God. How has *your* restoration been going?
- Who has tried to stop you? Which friends, or even family members have tried to distract you away from your spiritual life?
- Who has been your Darius, and given you unexpected encouragement?
- You are in a covenant relationship with God as much as Israel ever was. What 'visions' or insights into that relationship have you been given?
- And what of the future? You may want to spend time praying as you consider the next stage in your own life.

Read 2 Timothy 3:16—4:8.

                                                                          AC

Prayer missiles

For our struggle is not against flesh and blood, but against the rulers, against the authorities, against the powers of this dark world and against the spiritual forces of evil in the heavenly realms… With this in mind, be alert and always keep on praying.

Prayer has never been easy for me. In fact I remember praying once, 'Lord, please show me if it makes any difference at all!' God answered by using my crazy imagination! I was reading Ephesians 6 one evening, when I seemed to see those 'forces of evil in heavenly realms'. It was like watching an internal video. I could see myself sitting in my chair, launching prayers like missiles through the dark night sky and out towards the blazing light of heaven. As they zoomed away I realized they were under heavy enemy attack. Swarms of demons surrounded each one, hell-bent on destroying them before they reached their destination. Most of my feeble little missiles soon disappeared in pathetic puffs of smoke and flopped back to earth, defeated. Just a very few managed to twist and dodge through their attackers—heading straight on towards their target. Angels 'seemed' to reach down to collect the requests they carried, and hurried off with them to the Throne Room (Revelation 5:8; 8:4).

Imagination? Perhaps, but Satan is still around and dominates the airspace above (Ephesians 2:2). My private video show helped me realize that, if my prayers were important enough to warrant so much enemy attention, then launching these missiles was not a boring waste of time but the most vital thing I could possibly do.

The 'spiritual forces of evil' know that prayer is the one weapon that can defeat them. They are not concerned when they see us working to help others, but they are terrified once we begin to pray!

If we once realized how much good we could bring to others by praying for them, we would treat prayer as the most important activity in the day.

JRL

Vertical rockets

But when you pray, go into your room, close the door and pray to your Father, who is unseen. Then your Father, who sees what is done in secret, will reward you.

Not everyone finds it difficult to pray. Have you ever been in a small group or church meeting, and felt you could never compete with so many magnificent pray-ers! Their words flow so effortlessly—but are their sizzling missiles actually any more successful than your jerky, breathless efforts?

If the enemy can't stop us from praying he makes us so good at it he can tempt us to use prayer as a way of impressing others. We may not have Pharisees, accompanied by brass bands (v. 2), in our churches nowadays but many people long to feel important or respected for their spiritual power or special relationship with God.

The enemy also feels quite safe if we use prayer as an alternative to preaching. I once belonged to a house group where the leader encouraged us to share our 'prayer needs' and then prayed at length for each of us, saying in detail what she thought we ought to do and where we had gone wrong! We couldn't discuss or challenge her opinions because she appeared to be addressing the Almighty—but was she really? Perhaps, if we were all really honest, we might admit quite a few of our prayer missiles are fired horizontally rather than vertically!

Personally I find it far easier to pray when I am with one or two others; I concentrate better and find the whole activity more stimulating. I have several friends, however, who find other people a distraction when they want to pray. So is Jesus saying that we should only pray on our own? (v. 6) No, he just wants us to know that, whether we are praying by ourselves, or with thousands, we only ever have an audience of one.

Lord, please make yourself more real to me. Grow my faith so I can see and hear you with my spirit.

JRL

Boring babbling

And when you pray, do not keep on babbling like pagans, for they think they will be heard because of their many words.

Does prayer ever bore God? For years I worked my way, dutifully, through a long list of names every day but my mind was already on the day ahead. I was merely repeating the same set of words for each person: 'Lord bless… be with… help…'. I was bored, even if God was not! My prayers were not creative or spontaneous; they had become a mindless chore like cleaning my teeth.

To be effective we must *mean* our 'missiles', and sometimes a drastic change in our 'launching' methods helps considerably. I began using my computer when I prayed for other people (but pen and paper would be just as effective). Avoiding my old clichés 'bless… help… be with…', I made myself write down a few words beside each person's name, asking for one specific thing, which had to be different every day. Several times a year I read back through my prayer file and see, with astonishment, how God has answered so many of those short requests.

Another way I 'babble' (v. 7) is when I'm worried—perhaps about someone I love or a situation in my own life. I mutter away internally all day, while I forget appointments, burn the supper and drive in a dangerous daze. I try to kid myself I'm 'praying without ceasing', but I have a nasty feeling the enemy is not deceived! Effective prayer missiles are powered by faith. If we simply go on and on asking God to do something to help us without really trusting him to do it in his way and in his time, then we are not praying; we are merely using prayer as a vehicle to carry our worry!

Jesus says the Father knows what we need before we ask (v. 8) but it is the action of praying that releases the blessing. We do not have to tell him what to do, praying simply aligns our will with his.

JRL

Powered by anger

'But I tell you who hear me: Love your enemies, do good to those who hate you, bless those who curse you, pray for those who mistreat you.'

While some of our unsuccessful prayer missiles may be powered by worry, they are just as unsuccessful when fuelled by anger. If someone hurts us badly or makes our lives a misery, we know the Lord commands us to pray for them so we mutter: 'Lord, discipline him… may this new relationship make them both miserable… make her see my point of view.' But that kind of praying was not what Jesus meant (v. 28)! He wanted us to pray blessings (good things) down on the people who ruin our lives. Satanists stick pins in effigies that represent their 'difficult people' and attempt to curse them with bad things; Jesus wants us to do the exact opposite. He gives forgiveness the highest possible status because by refusing to forgive we lay ourselves and our prayer missiles wide open to enemy attack.

When you've been badly hurt Christian friends always urge: 'Forgive, let all your anger go', but it isn't as easy as that! Forgiving is something we have to keep on doing, over and over again—but it starts the moment we *choose* to forgive. We feel we've failed when those angry feelings keep coming back but all we have to do is *choose* to forgive yet again. It is only when we choose *not* to forgive that our missiles nosedive.

Negative prayers share the same fate. Most of us know we could be such good Christians if only God would remove one particular person! So we decide to 'pray them out'. 'Make him change jobs', we pray; 'move house… find another church.' Unfortunately, loving our VDPs (Very Difficult People) means accepting and encouraging them, not trying to manipulate God into making life more comfortable for us by removing them!

Prayer is about getting up above the world and our little human concerns so God can show us his bigger picture.

JRL

Discouragement

And blessed is he, whosoever shall not be offended in me.

My little granddaughter died last month after I had prayed long and hard for her healing. Naturally I began wondering, 'Were all those prayer missiles a waste of time? Perhaps I didn't have enough faith or had I sinned?' Doubts buzzed in my head until I remembered the enemy stops our missiles before they are launched when he uses a weapon called Discouragement. He loves condemnation too! When our prayers are not answered in the way we expect, he tells us it was 'all our fault'. So I agreed with him, my faith *is* weak and I *do* sin but no one has to be perfect to pray—just forgiven!

Yet I'm still left with the pain of having my agonized prayers apparently disregarded. Was that how John the Baptist was feeling (v. 19)? When the dungeon door first slammed on John he probably felt confident that Jesus would miraculously release him. Ever since he was a baby, John had sensed his destiny was to help the Messiah, and God had made it clear that his cousin Jesus was the One they had all been expecting for hundreds of years (John 1:26–34). He also knew that the scriptures foretold that the Messiah would set captives free (Isaiah 61:1); so surely Jesus would rescue him so they could get on with the job of setting up his kingdom? But Jesus never came, and John's last recorded words are full of doubt and despair (v. 20).

It is easy to believe in God's love and power when he answers all our prayers with a 'yes' and everything is going well. But it is in those dark dungeons of adversity where real faith either grows or dies completely. The choice is ours!

God didn't answer my prayers with a 'yes' so I can either feel 'offended' and not bother to pray for God's healing on future occasions. Or I can release all the good things he wants to bring into painful situations by continuing to pray anyway.

JRL

Just a look

So Moses made a bronze snake and put it up on a pole. Then when anyone was bitten by a snake and looked at the bronze snake, he lived.

I don't like snakes but this is one of my favourite passages on prayer in the whole Bible. The victims didn't have to crawl to God, make long speeches or costly promises—just a look of faith was enough to save their lives (v. 9). For years I struggled with a terrible sense of guilt over prayer and books on the subject only made me feel worse! Then I heard Joyce Huggett say, 'Pray as you can and not as you can't', and I was totally released.

Sometimes I can pray by using my own words, psalms, or the beautiful prayers written by other people; but when words don't seem to work I no longer feel a failure. When someone asks me to pray for them, or I find myself thinking about a friend, I just picture myself holding them by the hand. Then I look up and say, 'Lord, they need your help.'

For some mysterious reason God seems to limit himself to working through the prayers of humans like us, but it is not our words or the time we spend praying that matters; he just needs that look of faith. I love the story of King Jehoshaphat who, when faced by an invading army, prayed, 'O, our God… we do not know what to do, but our eyes are upon you' (2 Chronicles 20:12).

Two people who love and understand each other communicate in all kinds of different ways. Various messages can be conveyed by a glance across a crowded room; at other times they may talk for hours; write long letters when they are separated; or dump their painful feelings on one another. God wants us to communicate with him like that too, so why do we make prayer so complicated?

God hears us the instant we hit the 'H' of HELP! The 'ELP' is unnecessary.

                                            JRL

Drainpipes

*As the eyes of a maid look to the hand of her mistress, so our eyes
look to the Lord our God.*

'Tell me a story about Lady Fladgate…' As a child I often visited
Mrs Walster. She had been 'in service' and loved to tell me about
the grand dinner parties her mistress used to hold. 'She had ten of
us maids waiting at table, but never spoke her orders; she controlled
us all by her eyebrow and her first finger! If we didn't keep our eyes
on her all the time we were out of a job next morning.'

Prayer is not only about asking God to do what we want; it also
means allowing him to do what *he* wants. He needs our hands to
love and care for people down here on earth but he can only use us
effectively if, like Lady Fladgate's maids, we keep watching him
attentively.

Once I was driving to speak at a meeting when I was caught in
an awful motorway 'logjam'. Hopelessly late, I arrived at the church
steaming with stress. 'Please pray for me!' I said to the organizer. 'Sit
down,' she replied gently, 'and let me impart the peace of Jesus to
you.' Shutting the vestry door on the waiting congregation, she put
her hand on my shoulder and, as we sat in total silence, I began to
feel the peace pouring into me, just as if she had been a drainpipe
conveying the refreshing water of life right into my spirit!

We can all be drainpipes, silently imparting any of the qualities of
Jesus (love, strength, joy, wisdom) to others without hassling over
words. Drainpipes don't have to *do* anything; they just need to keep
open at the top (our relationship with Jesus) and open at the
bottom (our relationship with other people). They also have to
make sure rubbish doesn't clog them up in between!

---

*Lord, use me as a drainpipe today; flow through me into the people
you long to touch and comfort.*

JRL

Psalm 150 (NIV)

Praise the Lord

Let everything that has breath praise the Lord.

In church recently the final hymn was an old favourite, 'To God be the glory'. The sun was shining through the windows; I had just finished leading the intercessions—something I found difficult and had worried about for days—I was surrounded by friends and the sermon had been inspiring. So when it came to the chorus I sang with enormous feeling: 'Praise the Lord, praise the Lord, let the people rejoice…' (Fanny Crosby, 1820–1915).

It felt good and right to be singing God's praises. But what if I had been ill, or depressed? What if I had just lost a job—would I still feel like praising God? Because giving God praise actually has nothing to do with our personal feelings at the time—it has everything to do with who God is and who we are. Peter wrote, 'You are a chosen people, a royal priesthood, a holy nation, a people belonging to God, that you may declare the praises of him who called you out of darkness into his wonderful light' (1 Peter 2:9). Praise is our natural response, as believers, as God's chosen people, to the One who created us and saved us and made us his own.

In only six verses today's psalm tells us the where, the why and the how of praising God—and by whom. We praise him in his mighty heavens (v. 1). I love looking at the sky, especially when there are layers of cloud, for ever moving and changing; watching the sunset adding orange and red and turquoise to the grey and the blue. This huge expanse of space reminds me of our mighty God, who created everything in the universe. We praise him because he is our creator and redeemer (v. 2). And praise is not quiet or private; it is expressed openly and joyfully with music and (for the uninhibited) with dancing (vv. 3–5). In fact, 'everything that has breath'—everything that lives, exists to praise the Lord. Hallelujah!

Read Psalm 148 out loud.

MR

Pleasing to God

I will praise God's name in song and glorify him with thanksgiving. This will please the Lord more than an ox, more than a bull with its horns and hoofs.

Life is a bit more relaxed in our house in the mornings since my husband retired and we no longer live 'over the shop'. There is time to browse through the newspaper after breakfast—but sometimes I wonder why I do this. So many of the reports and articles seem to delight in being critical—looking only at the negatives in a person or an issue. We have become a nation of critics, which is sad because praise is something that adds to the quality of life.

One of the first things I learned about teaching children was the importance of praise. I taught five-year-olds struggling to learn to write. First, you looked for the good things in a piece of writing and gave enough praise to give pleasure and confidence. Then you could point out what needed to be improved without leaving the child discouraged. We all thrive on praise. One of the amazing things our verse tells us today is that God is pleased when we praise him! Our praise gives almighty God more pleasure than anything else.

When this psalm was written, God's people thought the way to please him was to give him expensive sacrifices. Perhaps the equivalent thinking today is that we need to earn God's approval by being better Christians. In Isaiah 43 God reminds the children of Israel of the many ways he had guided and protected them because they were his chosen people, 'the people I formed for myself that they may proclaim my praise' (Isaiah 43:21).

And praise is catching. In a psalm in praise of God's goodness, David says, 'I will extol the Lord at all times, his praise will always be on my lips… let the afflicted hear and rejoice' (Psalm 34:1–2).

Praise the Lord joyfully today—and help change any critical attitudes you hear to ones of praise!

MR

Praise—for he chose us

Praise be to the God and Father of our Lord Jesus Christ, who has blessed us in the heavenly realms with every spiritual blessing in Christ. For he chose us… to be holy and blameless in his sight.

I can remember, as a child, the tension of standing waiting to be 'chosen' by a team leader when we were getting ready to play rounders. The delight of being chosen first—and the ignominy of being left to the last has stayed in my memory. Paul, in his letter to the Ephesians, begins by praising God for all the spiritual blessings we have through Jesus—because God chose us to be his people.

God chose us—not because we have the potential to be good players in his team, but because he wants to bless us. No wonder this whole passage is a song of praise to our God and Father. We so often think that we 'decided to become a Christian', and we pray for those we know and love to 'give their lives to Christ'. How, then, does this fit with what Paul is saying so emphatically? Jesus also said to his disciples, 'You did not choose me but I chose you' (John 15:16).

Too often we can go through life thinking that we have chosen to serve God and to do his work. Paul himself originally thought he was doing the right thing for God when he travelled around persecuting and throwing in prison those who were believers in Jesus. But his life was turned around when Jesus confronted him on the road to Damascus (Acts 9:1–19). Paul, in his letter to the Galatian churches writes, 'God, who set me apart from birth and called me by his grace, was pleased to reveal his Son in me…' (Galatians 1:15–16).

God has chosen us from our very beginnings, but it is when we realize this that our lives are changed, and we enjoy that peace and assurance which are God's gifts to us.

God works for the good of those who love him, who have been called… (Romans 8:28).

MR

Following Jesus

The whole crowd of disciples began joyfully to praise God in loud voices.

Jesus was riding into Jerusalem surrounded by his disciples, who were praising God in loud voices. They had already seen Jesus perform many miracles—they must have been quite sure this miracle worker would carry on doing the same when he got to Jerusalem. Jesus had already explained to them that he had to go to Jerusalem where he would be mocked, insulted and killed (Luke 18:31–34). They hadn't really understood what he was saying then, and now Jesus' words seemed to be forgotten in the joy and excitement of the moment.

Jesus had planned this journey carefully. He had arranged for the donkey to be available for him. By riding in on a donkey he was claiming to be the promised Messiah, God's anointed king: 'Rejoice greatly, O Daughter of Zion! Shout, Daughter of Jerusalem! See, your king comes to you, righteous and having salvation, gentle and riding on a donkey, on a colt, the foal of a donkey. (Zechariah 9:9)

Jesus knew he was going to Jerusalem to die.

His disciples may have had some misgivings, but once surrounded by the cheering crowd they joined in with everyone else. A week later they were no longer singing praises to God—their Lord had been crucified. They had run away to hide, afraid and lost. Sheep without their shepherd. It wasn't until they met the risen Christ that they began to understand the significance of his death and rising again to new life.

There are times when we are like those disciples. It is great when everything is going well and we are surrounded by other believers. But what about those times in life when following Jesus isn't quite so easy, when God doesn't seem to be answering our cries for help? We can feel just as lost and frightened as those disciples. It is at these times that we have to hold on to God's promises. 'Never will I leave you; never will I forsake you' (Hebrews 13:5) is one that is easy to learn and recall when you need reassurance of God's presence with you.

Look up 1 Peter 5:7; Matthew 6:25, 26.

MR

Praising in prison

About midnight Paul and Silas were praying and singing hymns to God, and the other prisoners were listening to them.

Paul and Silas had travelled to Philippi in answer to what they were sure was God's call (Acts 16:9). But things soon began to go wrong. They had been followed around by a slave girl who had kept shouting, 'These men are servants of the most High God…' Finally, in exasperation, Paul cast out the spirit of divination in the girl. Her owners, furious at their loss of income from her fortune-telling, dragged Paul and Silas to face the magistrates for 'throwing the city into an uproar'. They were stripped, flogged and thrown into prison.

They had obeyed God's call to go to Macedonia and here they were in prison! Their reaction to everything going wrong was to sing and praise God—what a witness to the other prisoners. Do read the rest of the story.

I once knew a man who was a prisoner in his own body. He had an incurable illness which meant he was losing his ability to move. He was a heavy man and the only times he could leave his hospital bed were when someone strong enough could lift him into his wheelchair. Cyril was a radiant Christian. His whole life was a song of praise to his Lord. He was sure God wanted him in that hospital so he could bring the love of Jesus to the other men in his ward. Occasionally he was able to get to our church, with the aid of friends with a car he could be squeezed into. Young and old in that congregation were always happy to be near Cyril. His funeral was a joyful affair. Cyril was no longer imprisoned in a body that would not work. He was with his Lord. In the front of the church that day there were several wheelchairs—men from his ward in the hospital had come to see why Cyril had been so happy.

Loving Father, help me to keep praising you, no matter what happens.
MR

Unexpected healing

'Silver and gold I do not have, but what I have I give you. In the name of Jesus Christ of Nazareth, walk.' … instantly the man's feet and ankles became strong… Then he went with them into the temple courts, walking and jumping and praising God.

Giving money to people in need was something every devout Jew considered right, and beggars would make sure they were seen by those going to the temple to pray. This particular man was a cripple from birth; every day he was carried to a place outside one of the temple gates where he could ask for money.

Someone I know always carried a pocketful of coins to give to those begging for money on the streets of London. She knew they would be there; she trusted they really were in need, and she was ready to be asked. Peter and John, who went daily to the temple to pray, would not have been surprised to be asked for money by this man. They could have had some coins ready to give him (see Acts 2:45), but Peter knew he could give this man something far better— he could offer healing.

'In the name of Jesus Christ of Nazareth, walk.' Peter took hold of the man's hand to help him to his feet, and immediately he could not only stand but walk and leap for joy. As he went with Peter and John into the temple courts he praised God, and those nearby recognized him as the crippled beggar who sat by the gate, and were amazed to see him walking and praising God.

The next day Peter and John had to give an account for this act of kindness to the rulers and elders of the city. 'It is by the name of Jesus Christ… whom you crucified but whom God raised from the dead, that this man stands before you healed… Salvation is found in no one else.' The lame man was healed, but Peter longed for those listening to see that Jesus could give them total healing—salvation.

Read the whole chapter.

MR

Praising God together

They broke bread in their homes and ate together
with glad and sincere hearts, praising God and enjoying
the favours of all the people.

What a perfect picture this is of the early Church in Jerusalem. The Holy Spirit had been given to the disciples, as promised by Jesus before he ascended to heaven. 'You will receive power when the Holy Spirit comes on you, and you will be my witnesses in Jerusalem, and in all Judea and Samaria, and to the ends of the earth' (Acts 1:8).

The Christians in Jerusalem would have become the focus of attention to others because of the event of Pentecost (Acts 1:5–10). Every day the believers went to the temple—taking part in the worship of God in the accepted manner. Then they ate together in their homes 'with glad and sincere hearts, praising God and enjoying the favour of all the people'. I can almost hear you sigh and wish your church were as perfect as this!

Eating together, especially in the East, has always been a sign of fellowship. In our busy Western lifestyles today, families rarely do this. Many children, when they start school, have to learn how to sit at a table and eat together with their friends. Having friends and neighbours in to join you for a meal is one of the most enjoyable ways of spending an evening that I know, because there is time to talk. I often wonder whether the Big Brother programmes were so popular because we no longer 'look over the garden fence' at our neighbour. Neighbourhood communities are rare—so what we see on TV has become our neighbourhood.

Christians who meet together and clearly enjoy each other's company—whether it is in church or in a home—will attract others, just as they did when the disciples first broke bread together.

What about inviting a neighbour in for coffee today?

                                                                MR

Revolution

Therefore, I urge you, brothers, in view of God's mercy, to offer your bodies as living sacrifices, holy and pleasing to God—this is your spiritual act of worship. Do not conform any longer to the pattern of this world, but be transformed by the renewing of your mind. Then you will be able to test and approve what God's will is—his good, pleasing and perfect will.

It is time to delve into Romans. Paul's exhaustive defence of the gospel in his letter to the Roman Christians has proved to be life-changing for countless people, and fundamental to Christian theology. Mind you, that doesn't make it easy to read. Paul's brilliant mind and addiction to long sentences have taxed the best of readers. However, let us sally forth undaunted and attempt to mine the last quarter of Romans for its treasures.

Like all good letters, these latter words only make sense because of the ones that came before. The 'therefore' which begins our quotation above refers to the rock-solid basis Paul has already built for faith in Jesus. He has been meticulous in establishing the implications of Jesus' life, death and resurrection. He has emphasized our dependence on the grace of God, as his gift and our security. So now he can call us to respond wholeheartedly to God's generosity and love, by throwing ourselves into his arms, totally dependent on him, and as vulnerable as a sacrifice. This, says Paul, is what worship is.

But don't stop there! Paul urges us to get our thinking in line with God's, because then we will know what to do. How many times have we longed for God to write the answer in the sky when facing a difficult decision? Here's how to do it, says Paul. Allow God to transform your mind; then you will know.

This is revolutionary stuff for our independent 21st-century attitudes. Worship, dependence, sacrifice, the will of God—not words we read too often in the newspapers. But Paul insists they are the place to start in our response to God.

What do these words mean to you?

                                                              DA

Be sober!

Do not think of yourself more highly than you ought, but rather think of yourself with sober judgment, in accordance with the measure of faith God has given you. Just as each of us has one body with many members, and these members do not all have the same function, so in Christ we who are many form one body, and each member belongs to all the others.

Interesting that we have the word 'sober' here. What is 'sober judgment'? What would 'drunken judgment' be? I suppose that too much drink distorts our perceptions and behaviour, so perhaps the self-awareness Paul is encouraging is based on realism. But don't many of us start with the opposite problem when judging ourselves? Often we women think too little of ourselves rather than too highly. Many of us struggle mightily with low esteem and feelings of inadequacy. But wherever we begin, Paul's advice is the same: Look at what God has gifted you for within the body of Christ—the 'measure of faith'—and use his power to do it.

This is easier said than done. Despite our mental assent to Paul's following words, that we all belong together in Christ and have various functions, we tie ourselves in knots rather than enjoy getting on with our own particular function. We fall prey to envying others' gifts, or to doubting our own. We can't quite believe that we too have abilities that others need, and get embarrassed if our church or home group ever threatens one of those 'find your gift' questionnaires. Surely not me? I can't possibly acknowledge something positive and useful in the way I am made! Much too scary! Ask me for a list of my faults and I can do it enthusiastically. I can disqualify myself for useful service in two minutes flat, no problem.

You can see why Paul had to encourage 'sober judgment'. He just wanted us to see ourselves clearly: as dependent, joyful, grace-filled children of God, gifted for service to one another and confidently discharging that service in the power of God.

Read Zephaniah 3:16, 17.

DA

All you need is love

Love must be sincere. Hate what is evil; cling to what is good. Be devoted to one another in brotherly love. Honour one another above yourselves.

With all the talk and singing about love, especially in our relationship-obsessed Western world, you would have thought we had this love thing sussed. After all, we have had 2,000 years since Paul wrote these words to get it right. But Paul's words are as cuttingly relevant today as they ever were. We still need to be reminded that love must be sincere. Few of us have not been hurt by the insincere kind in one way or another, or indeed, have not caused hurt ourselves. We all know that when we are truly loved, then we flourish in confidence and security. We also know that when we are unsure of love, we wither.

Relationships cannot blossom without real love, whether in family, church or community. We all need the love that is committed to the best for us, and will stick by us through thick and thin. So Paul's challenge to the Romans reaches us too. Can we give real love to each other? Can we be 'devoted' to one another? Can we disentangle ourselves from selfishness and fear, and offer sincere love without restraint?

I wonder how you react to the injunction to honour each other above ourselves. On low-esteem days, I think I do that in an unhealthy I-am-but-a-worm way. On confident days, I think I am anyone's equal. Both these approaches are missing the point. Paul wants us to live in the good kingdom of God, where evil is shunned with passion. In the kingdom, we are all equal recipients of God's boundless love and grace, so are free to offer love and grace to each other. Here, we are free to honour others with joy because we have no need to judge whether they are worth it. They too have been bought with a great price.

Dear Father, help me to know your love so I may offer mine to others. Amen.

Read 1 Corinthians 13.

DA

Romans 12:11–13 (NIV)

Get real!

Never be lacking in zeal, but keep your spiritual fervour, serving the Lord. Be joyful in hope, patient in affliction, faithful in prayer. Share with God's people who are in need. Practise hospitality.

Wouldn't you love to be like this? Wouldn't you love to put a tick by all of Paul's requirements here? Perhaps I am doing you an injustice; perhaps the ticks are down already. I just haven't met you yet. The Christians I know, however wonderful, all have their off-days, and sometimes need reminding what loving means.

I suspect that we all find some loving more difficult than others. For example, some find hospitality comes quite naturally, while others get caught up in what people will criticize when they walk in the door. A salutary story I heard told of a newly married couple who were so embarrassed at the messy state of their flat that they kept a friend talking on the doorstep for an hour rather than invite him in. The wife recounted the incident with regret, recognizing that she had put her own pride before the warmth and welcome of friendship. Does it actually matter if people see our unkempt nests? It might be quite reassuring for them.

Perhaps it's rather the thought of consistent zealous enthusiasm for Jesus that daunts you. Or maybe you are slightly perplexed by those who happily spend hours in prayer, when you struggle to find a sentence or two. Perhaps you have got the hang of holding possessions loosely, so willingly share them with others. Perhaps not. Then there is the real test—that joyful, patient attitude to life and trials. Who among us can claim that one as a feather in our cap?

These things are true challenges for all of us, in one way or another. We need to remember to face them with grace: God's grace for each one of us. This isn't actually a checklist of attributes. It's just the good things God wants to grow in us.

Dear Father, please fill me with your Spirit, and grow your love in me. Amen.

DA

Romans 12:17–19 (NIV)

Mission impossible

Do not repay anyone evil for evil. Be careful to do what is right in the eyes of everybody. If it is possible, as far as it depends on you, live at peace with everyone. Do not take revenge, my friends, but leave room for God's wrath, for it is written: 'It is mine to avenge; I will repay,' says the Lord.

I don't know about you, but I think that here Paul puts his finger on one of the hardest demands the Christian life makes. This not-paying-back-people-for-wrong-things-they-do is so very difficult. When I or someone I love are sinned against, everything in me automatically screams out for revenge, no matter how large or small the offence. She hurt me, so I am justified in hurting her. She deserves it. It's only fair.

Yet deep down I know that the cycle of destruction never solves anything. I have seen this many times in my children's relationships. Two injured parties come yelling for my attention, sporting bruises of mind or body, and demand my adjudication. I learned very early on that it is practically impossible to judge fairly unless I have seen the fight—and even then I may not know all the facts. Each child is fully and passionately convinced of the rightness of their respective cause. Each has attempted to repay evil for evil, and it has resulted in relationship breakdown and spiralling injury.

God clearly calls us to leave the adjudication to him for the unfair ways we are treated in life. He alone knows all the facts and he alone is qualified to judge. He wants us to take the gigantic step of trusting him to avenge what needs avenging. He wants us to be free: to forgive and to be at peace with all as far as we can. He encourages us to let go of our demands and let him deal with the evil. I guess he also knows just how difficult this is.

Our Father, forgive me my sins, as I forgive those who sin against me. Amen.

Read Matthew 5:7.

DA

Give unto Caesar...

*This is also why you pay taxes, for the authorities are God's
servants, who give their full time to governing. Give everyone
what you owe him: if you owe taxes, pay taxes; if revenue, then
revenue; if respect, then respect; if honour, then honour.*

Paul may have finished with complex theology in Romans for now,
but he certainly hasn't finished with the challenges. As if the injunction to leave vengeance to God is not hard enough, here comes
another tall order. Which do you find hardest—paying taxes or paying honour? Paul makes no allowance for the possibility that your
taxes may be going to a corrupt government, or even a persecuting
one. Presumably the authority in question was Roman through and
through, and was no friend to the Christians Paul was addressing.
Paul is convinced that authority exists because it is established by
God. Paul is unequivocal that to rebel against authority in these
matters is to rebel against God (v. 2).

This raises some tricky questions. Is there ever a case for with-
holding taxes, for example? What if the authorities are blatantly
pulling society apart rather than doing it good? Surely many
governors do not have a clue that they are God's servants, let
alone govern in a godly way? Paul by-passed these issues completely, but perhaps it goes back to that trusting-God thing.
Perhaps we can submit to even rotten authorities because we know
that ultimately God is in charge, and that we can trust him with
our money.

What about honour and respect, then? Do we talk about our
councillors and politicians with either? What about those in authority in our churches? To whom do we *owe* honour, whether or not we
think they have earned it? If God has put them over us, then we
must trust him with the outcome of that. We are certainly not going
to call the best out of anyone if we deride and complain about their
leadership. We are all subject to authority somewhere, and have to
learn submission.

---

*Any conscience-pricking questions that occur to you from today's
reading?*

                                                                    DA

Do as you are told

*The commandments, 'Do not commit adultery', 'Do not murder',
'Do not steal', 'Do not covet', and whatever other commandment
there may be, are summed up in this one rule: 'Love your
neighbour as yourself.' Love does no harm to its neighbour.
Therefore love is the fulfilment of the law.*

We had a little competition in our church service recently to see
who could remember the Ten Commandments. Maybe some people
were too modest to speak up, but as a congregation we struggled.
Perhaps we should have copied Paul and said, 'They are all about
love!'

Later, the sermon spelt out why Jesus himself extended already
difficult commands to impossible levels: the 'anyone who looks at a
woman lustfully has already committed adultery with her in his
heart' (Matthew 5:28) principle. (Or man, I assume.) None of this
outward show business. God wants integrity.

So how do you react when told not to do something? Does it
depend who tells you? Is there any Eve-in-Eden part of you that
doubts God when he speaks? When God says 'Do not covet', does
he include you and me, or can we actually envy our neighbour's
lifestyle, personality or husband because we are only human after all
and surely God won't notice? I sometimes think that the times we
long desperately for God's presence are more than equalled by the
times we hope fervently he is busy elsewhere.

Of course when we are thinking clearly we know that the Ten
Commandments make personal, moral and social sense. Community
just will not work without rules, any more than tiddlywinks will.
But when it comes to our own secret dreams and desires, it is con-
venient to wonder whether a little bit of stealing, murder and lust
really isn't going to upset the balance very much…

We are indeed all human and so we are all fallible, every single one
of us. But Paul, like Jesus, calls us away from the edge and beckons us
towards real love. I suppose they don't want us, or others, to miss out
on the best.

Read John 15:9–17.

DA

Best clothes

Let us behave decently, as in the daytime, not in orgies and drunkenness, not in sexual immorality and debauchery, not in dissension and jealously. Rather, clothe yourselves with the Lord Jesus Christ, and do not think about how to gratify the desires of the sinful nature.

We're not off the hook yet! Paul is determined to spell out the differences between living inside the kingdom of God and living outside it. He wants his readers to immerse themselves in the good stuff of the kingdom, and not be fooled by the antics of evil. He is not going to let us get away with thinking that some things are OK when they are not.

What do you think of when Paul refers to the 'sinful nature'? Something kind of greedy and grasping, ultimately selfish, never satisfied and a bit slimy perhaps? Do you recognize it in yourself when it tries to get hold of you and drag you away from Jesus? Some of the forbidden territory Paul describes above would not be a temptation for me. But some of it would. And I am not going to tell you which because that would distract us both into wondering how I might go about gratifying it, when Paul's whole point is not to think about that.

Yes, Paul wants to label the darkness for what it is (v. 12). But having done that, he wants us to focus our thoughts on Jesus. He wants us to clothe ourselves with Jesus—to put on all the fantastic goodness of Jesus that will completely obliterate our slime. So how do you envisage that working? Choosing to put on real love, kindness, patience and self-control like a favourite jacket, perhaps?

My high school had as its theme Philippians 4:8: 'Whatever is true, whatever is noble, whatever is right, whatever is pure, whatever is lovely, whatever is admirable—if anything is excellent or praiseworthy—think about such things.' It was read at every opportunity till I was tired of hearing it. Now, I am beginning to realize just how vital it is.

Read Ephesians 5:8–16.

DA

Vegetables, Madam?

*Accept him whose faith is weak, without passing judgment on
disputable matters… The man who eats everything must not look
down on him who does not, and the man who does not eat
everything must not condemn the man who does, for God has
accepted him.*

Hands up, all you vegetarians out there. There are a lot of us these
days. Do you ever feel condemned by others for not eating meat? The
only major incredulity I have come across was in Australia, where no
one could understand why I didn't want to eat the produce from their
back few acres. And as for refusing the famous Aussie barbeque—
how could I? But then, how about you carnivores? Do you have to
defend your enjoyment of meat from us tofu-eaters?

Paul was not quite addressing our current situation in his letter
to the Romans. He was probably concerned by the disagreements
arising between those who had forsaken the Jewish laws on diet and
food, and those who still held to them. The former were presumably
enjoying their new-found freedom in Christ, while the latter were
perhaps not sure whether salvation by faith meant they could chuck
out their cookbooks.

But Paul was not concerned with who was right and who was
wrong. What bothered him was the arguing. He didn't want the
Roman Christians to be wrangling over things that were not that
important. He wanted them to accept each other, warts and all, and
not be trapped into judging each other.

How frighteningly easy it is for us to get hot under the collar
about 'disputable matters'! What does your Christian community
fall out over? Is it worth it? What doctrines do you hold dear that
Paul would raise his eyebrows over, and declare 'disputable'?
Obviously the central beliefs of Christianity are non-negotiable. But
we must all beware of including our own pet passions as well, and
thereby casting condemnation on fellow believers.

---

*Dear Father, help me to see the plank in my own eye before trying to
take the speck out of my sister's. Amen.*

                                                                    DA

Loving food

*Let us therefore make every effort to do what leads to peace and
to mutual edification. Do not destroy the work of God for the sake
of food. All food is clean, but it is wrong for a man to eat
anything that causes someone else to stumble… everything that
does not come from faith is sin.*

I don't think Paul is talking about chocolate here, but you never
know. If he is, then I suspect that I am more likely to cause myself
to stumble rather than anyone else. But then, I suppose the restraint
principle still applies, for we are called to love each other as we love
ourselves…

This is all about love really, isn't it? Paul is just hammering out how
loving each other applies to things like what we eat. If your sister in
Christ is getting upset by your behaviour, then change it. For the
Romans, it was food laws. For us, it may be something different, but
keep the love principle paramount. Who among us would willingly
destroy the kingdom of God for the sake of something unimportant?
In order to build the kingdom of God on earth, we must watch our
actions. We must be prepared to lay aside our personal preferences if
necessary. This reminds me of the missionary who drank the cup of
water offered to him, including the frog at the bottom, rather than
offend the man who had given it to him. Kingdom first, kingdom first.
And didn't Jesus promise us that food and clothing, the basics of life,
would be ours anyway if we put his kingdom and righteousness first in
our priorities (Matthew 6:33)?

'If you confuse others by making a big issue over what they eat or
don't eat, you're no longer a companion with them in love, are you?
These, remember, are persons for whom Christ died… Don't you
dare let a piece of God-blessed food become an occasion of soul-
poisoning!' (from Romans 15, *The Message*).

What does it mean for you to seek God's kingdom first?

DA

Good receivers

May the God of hope fill you with all joy and peace as you trust in him, so that you may overflow with hope by the power of the Holy Spirit.

After all the hard-hitting challenges of the last few days, it is a relief to come across a 'kettle verse': one we can copy out and stick to the kettle for encouragement. This wonderful blessing that Paul bestows on the Romans is what we all want: joy, peace, trust and hope.

So how do we get there? Becoming a Christian does not guarantee us a hassle-free existence. Indeed, Jesus promised us 'trouble' in this world (John 16:33), and all of us know what 'trouble' looks like. Some face persecution of the harshest kinds for their faith in Jesus. The Christian life is not easy.

This is not to do with personality, either. Some people naturally have an optimistic outlook, some the opposite. This is to do with true hope that is based on reality, and joy that lasts when happiness is elusive.

In John 16, Jesus also said that our peace is *in him*—not in our circumstances, or in the world, or in ourselves. Jesus is the key. We must turn to him for the whole lot: for meaning to life, for salvation, for help today and tomorrow, for a certain eternity, for joy and peace. Paul's prayer is that we should be so full of joy and peace that we overflow. Paul wants us to have a rock-solid basis to our whole lives. So that despite events, we will still know the underpinning security of being a loved and precious child of God.

In case that seems out of reach, I am convinced that we only know this security when we trustingly receive it. This is not something we have to work up for ourselves. It is in 'the power of the Holy Spirit' alone. So all we have to do is receive it…

Can you take time today to receive joy and peace from God, by his Holy Spirit? How often do you need to do this?

DA

Money talks

For Macedonia and Achaia were pleased to make a contribution for the poor among the saints in Jerusalem. They were pleased to do it, and indeed they owe it to them. For if the Gentiles have shared in the Jews' spiritual blessings, they owe it to the Jews to share with them their material blessings.

What Paul really wanted to do was to go to Rome and meet the Christians there. But before he could go, he had to take to Jerusalem the money the Gentile churches in Macedonia and Achaia had collected. The predominantly Jewish believers in Jerusalem were struggling to survive, and needed the help.

There is a lovely balance here between the spiritual and material. Paul sees both as absolutely necessary. He is clearly delighted to be able to support the Jews materially after they have given to the Gentiles spiritually. The Jews are not embarrassed by their need, and neither is Paul hesitant to talk about money.

This does not compare well with Western society's attitude. Society says that money is the answer to life, and the more you have, the happier you will be. Christians can get caught in the trap of believing that, or alternatively of relegating our material needs as inferior to our spiritual ones. Of course, our relationship with Jesus is the most important thing for any of us. But Jesus was there at creation, and endorsed what had been made by becoming a living, breathing, eating human being. He too needed money to survive.

I am not quite sure why we get knotted up about money. It seems to have become a very personal thing that we have to talk about very carefully. Perhaps that is why Jesus talked about it so much! He wanted us to be free from worrying about it, and free to bless others with it, as the Gentile churches were through Paul.

The Jews and Gentiles willingly shared their spiritual and material blessings. Both are needed for the kingdom of God to grow. Let's do the same.

Read Malachi 3:8–12.

DA

Paul and women

I commend to you our sister Phoebe, a servant of the church in Cenchrea... Greet Priscilla and Aquila, my fellow-workers in Christ Jesus. They risked their lives for me... Greet Andronicus and Junias, my relatives who have been in prison with me. They are outstanding among the apostles, and they were in Christ before I was.

Paul closes his letter with a list of greetings to fellow Christians. After addressing believers as 'brothers' throughout Romans, it is fascinating to note just how many on his closing list are women! Read through chapter 16—it is the women who receive the biggest commendations. Junias, above, is a female name, so does this reference mean she was accepted as an apostle?

Some of Paul's writings have been criticized as anti-women, but this list seems to belie that. He calls Phoebe a 'servant of the church' which implies an official role—a deacon, perhaps? From the way Paul writes here, there is no implication that women are second-class, as people, as Christians, or as church workers.

Church denominations today have varied approaches towards women. The treatment of women has undoubtedly been a vexed question for the Church over the centuries, one which still rumbles on today. This has affected different women in different ways, and for some it has brought difficulty and pain. Whatever approach your church has, how do *you* see yourself before God? Do you see yourself as equal-but-different from men? Are there things you would do differently, in spiritual terms, if you were a man? If so, why? I don't pretend to know all the answers, but I believe the questions are worth asking. Perhaps the most important question is this: As a Christian who is a woman, are you achieving your potential in Christ, or is anything inside you holding you back?

'There is neither Jew nor Greek, slave nor free, male nor female, for you are all one in Christ Jesus' (Galatians 3:28).

Dear Father, help me to enjoy and explore my position in Christ as the woman you have made me to be. Amen.

DA

Graceful obedience

Everyone has heard about your obedience, so I am full of joy over you; but I want you to be wise about what is good, and innocent about what is evil. The God of peace will soon crush Satan under your feet. The grace of our Lord Jesus be with you.

I don't know how you finish letters, but I would love someone to end one to me in praise of my obedience! Perhaps I should consider whether I have earned such admiration. If Paul was addressing a church community, what did their obedience mean? Did it mean that the Roman church had very happy leaders? If Paul was referring to their general obedience to the gospel, then they not only had happy leaders, but also an enthusiastic, vibrant faith that commended them to 'everyone'. Paul was happy about them and he hadn't even met them! What an enviable reputation.

But Paul still reminded them to keep watch. He encouraged them to throw themselves into the good stuff and totally avoid the bad. He wanted them to keep their good name. We live in many shades of grey, and we need to cultivate wisdom to know black from white. What is good? How do we celebrate the good things God has given us to enjoy, without compromising with evil? In our interwoven, interdependent world, this is not always easy to discern. We need to be sensitive to the inner prompting of the Holy Spirit, and ready with our obedience. Whether it's lifestyle, money-management, entertainment, church involvement—the list is endless—we must be honest with God about our motives and decisions. In the end, our God of peace will squelch evil out of existence. Not much point in aligning with it, then.

But all this is always, and in all ways, in the context of grace. Because of grace we can respond to anything God asks us to do. We are already free. We are already justified before him. God accepts us completely because of Jesus. From now on, it is an adventure.

Dear Father, help me to earn a good reputation, too. Amen.

DA

No one mourned

The Lord struck him [Jehoram] in the bowels with an incurable disease. In course of time, at the end of two years, his bowels came out because of the disease, and he died in great agony. His people made no fire in his honour, like the fires made for his ancestors.

These final chapters of 2 Chronicles are a rollercoaster of good and evil, leading to the dynasty's final decline. Jehoram's father, Jehoshaphat, had been an impressive, God-fearing king, though with weaknesses, in his failure to demolish the Canaanite shrines and his treaty with the king of Israel. Before he died he gave each of his sons gifts of silver and gold, and shared out the fortified cities in the country. Jehoram, the eldest, became king.

Once on the throne, the 32-year-old's first act was to kill all his brothers. Was he afraid of a revolt from their fortified cities? Was he greedy for their riches? Whatever his motive, sibling rivalry does not usually lead to murder! But this incident does encourage us to reflect on the quality of our relationships with our own brothers and sisters. I am aware that I have not talked with my brother for months; I can remedy that this week. It is not active estrangement —just neglect.

Jehoshaphat had failed to destroy the high places, built for Canaanite worship; Jehoram built new ones, and actively led his people to worship other gods. Apathy in one generation easily leads to apostasy (turning away from God) in another. Much evil during Jehoram's life led to much pain at the end—defeat at the hands of the Philistines, the capture of much of his family, the loss of his possessions, a very painful illness (bowel cancer, maybe?). It reminds me of Paul's warning: 'God is not mocked, for you reap whatever you sow. If you sow to your own flesh, you will reap corruption from the flesh' (Galatians 6:7, 8).

The saddest comment of all—when he died, 'he departed with no one's regrets'. What a grievous end!

What would you like as an epitaph?

RG

The power of two women

When Athaliah, Ahaziah's mother, saw that her son was dead, she set about to destroy all the royal family of the house of Judah. But Jehoshabeath, the king's daughter, took Joash son of Ahaziah, and stole him away from among the king's children who were about to be killed.

Jehoram's son Ahaziah was king for only a year. He was killed on a visit to his wounded relative Joram, king of Israel, with whom he had teamed up. Despite his evil behaviour, he was given a decent burial 'for they said, "He is the grandson of Jehoshaphat, who sought the Lord with all his heart"' (v. 9). It is sad when those who have a strong godly heritage abandon the faith.

With no strong male heir apparent, his wicked mother Athaliah —who was descended from Omri, an evil king of Israel—grabbed the reins of power and tried to exterminate the rest of the royal family of Judah. (Does this begin to sound like a fairy story? I first met this tale in the play *Athalie* when I studied French at school. But it is not fiction.) As her power grew, we begin to wonder how these strands of evil and murder could be cut.

But power does not have to be shown by throwing your weight around. It can be exercised secretly, as Jehoshabeath did. She was Ahaziah's sister or half-sister, and is the only example of a royal princess married to a high priest. Her quiet hiding away of the infant prince and his wet nurse postponed by more than two centuries the end of the royal family of Judah. Most of us are in some position of power—even when we feel that we're not! For a start, think what measure of control you have over your own life. Then think about the ways in which you have power over other situations or other people. Think about your motives, the ways you use your power, and its effects.

Lord, please help me to be more like Jehoshabeath, and not at all like Athaliah.

RG

One man's faithfulness

The whole assembly made a covenant with the king in the house of God. Jehoida said to them, 'Here is the king's son! Let him reign, as the Lord promised concerning the sons of David.'

Jehoida and Jehoshabeath—hardly names that would readily come to mind if we were asked to talk about married couples in the Bible! Yet they are key figures at this point in Judah's history. We have already seen Jehoshabeath's part in hiding the infant Joash away from his murderous grandmother. Six years later, Jehoida the high priest called together five key leaders and told them of his plan to depose Athaliah and to restore the rightful heir to the throne. Between them they went throughout the country and called together all the Levites and the leaders of the clans. The rest of this chapter tells us of the people's joy at Joash's coronation, of the death of Athaliah and the destruction of the temple of Baal.

It is always worth reading between the lines in biblical narrative. These are real people, even though they lived in a culture that is so different from our own. What was it like for them? How might we have behaved in that situation? Here are some of the qualities I see in Jehoida; some are obvious, some are implicit.

- *His patience:* He waited six years before he showed his hand. Would any small boy you know be easy to contain, confined to the temple precincts? My grandson wouldn't!
- *His courage* is apparent.
- *His wisdom* in all his actions.
- *His sensitivity:* He would have been unwise to make a move without being aware of the climate of opinion in the country.
- *His strategy:* His plans were carefully devised and executed.
- *His forward planning:* There was nothing haphazard in his actions.
- *His determination* to rout out Baal worship and—above all—to serve the Lord.

It was not just the king but God whom he was determined to put in his rightful place.

Lord, please show me what you want me to be and do in your kingdom.
                                                                          RG

Do it now!

Some time later Joash decided to restore the temple of the Lord.
He called together the priests and Levites and said to them, 'Go to
the towns of Judah and collect the money due annually from all
Israel, to repair the temple of your God. Do it now.' But the
Levites did not act at once.

Most passages of scripture offer us several different lessons. What theme from today's verses would you choose if you were writing these notes? We could concentrate on verse 2: 'Joash did what was right in the eyes of the Lord all the years of Jehoiada the priest.' Or we might focus on Joash's work in rebuilding the temple, and think about repairing broken lives.

I was caught by the phrase 'Do it now'. Maybe that is because of my own tendency to procrastinate! Many years into his reign, Joash decided to embark on a new project, to restore the temple which had fallen into disrepair and been looted during Athaliah's reign. Once committed to the task, he wanted to get on with it. 'Go and collect the money… Do it now… Why hasn't it been done?' I confess I find something a bit hypocritical about his new urgency, when he had waited for years to get the repairs under way. Was he feeling guilty about the delay, and pushing that guilt on to other people?

Procrastination is a deadly enemy. Its fruit is seen in missed deadlines, in wasted opportunities, in work done hurriedly and carelessly. If I have a job waiting from which I shrink, I often fiddle around doing other things—none of them efficiently. When I eventually tackle the 'difficult' task it is usually far easier than I had anticipated! 'Not yet, Lord' is a contradiction. He is not Lord if we are refusing to do what he asks for *now*. But we must not confuse procrastination with patience; it is disobedience, too, if I rush ahead when he says, 'Wait'.

Lord, please help me to distinguish between your 'do it now' and your
'wait'.

RG

Off with constraints!

They buried [Jehoiada] in the city of David among the kings,
because he had done good in Israel, and for God and his house...
[Joash] died; and they buried him in the city of David, but they
did not bury him in the tombs of the kings.

The priest was buried among the tombs, but the king himself was excluded in death. What had happened to this king, whose main project had been to oversee major repairs to the temple? There is a noticeable contrast in Joash before and after Jehoiada's death. As long as the old priest was alive, Joash followed the Lord. But when Jehoiada died, he turned to other advisers, and to Baal worship. When Jehoiada's son Zechariah rebuked the king, Joash murdered him. Clearly he made his own choices. But I have also been reflecting on the quality of Jehoiada's mentoring, and wonder if it was altogether as wise as it first appears.

Many of us are in some position of mentoring—as parents, teachers, counsellors, pastors, in personnel management. We want to help those who are under us to grow in skill and character, towards maturity. Jehoiada's lead in Joash's early years was vital, and he chose wives from Jerusalem (25:2) to ensure that the king would not revert to marriage into Athaliah's family. But I suspect that his strong control meant that Joash did not learn to make his own right decisions. When the leash was off, he broke away from God.

What does this say to us as mentors? One principle is 'Guide, but don't squeeze.' With our own children, we gave them as long a rope as we thought they could handle. We risked some wrong decisions, but I believe they learnt wisdom and independence. In their spiritual development, each one clearly asked Jesus into their lives when they were young. In their teenage years they did not always conform, but healthy roots bore fruit in adulthood. We thank God for that.

Pray by name for each person for whom you are responsible to teach,
train and guide.

RG

A patchy life

He did what was right in the eyes of the Lord, but not wholeheartedly.

'Good, but…' Amaziah's life is like the proverbial curate's egg—good in parts. He started well, executing only those who had murdered his father (24:25). Despite Joash's sin, they had no right to kill the king. Amaziah was careful to obey scripture, executing only the killers, not their offspring. So far, so good.

His next recorded act was to collect an army. He set about this methodically, conscripting all the men of Judah of fighting age. He seemed intent on war. Even 300,000 troops did not satisfy him, and he enrolled 100,000 mercenaries from Israel. At this point a prophet stepped in with a warning. 'Don't keep them, for God is not with them. However courageously you fight, you'll lose.' It is important that, whatever the nature of our battle, we fight it in God's way. Notice verse 8. We are usually quicker to remember God's power to help than his power to overthrow.

Amaziah was dismayed at the waste of the money he had already paid to the mercenaries, but to his credit he listened to the warning and dismissed his troops. In your life, have you ever had a tug-of-war between your conscience and financial gain? Which won? Pause now for a prayer: either thank God that he helped you to obey him or confess your greed. The mercenaries were furious at being sent away, and plundered many towns in their own country on their return trip. You might say, 'That was their choice, not Amaziah's.' True. But it was destruction that only happened because Amaziah hired them in the beginning. Have wrong actions in your life started a chain of events?

Amaziah's own army behaved even worse—prisoners of war were sent hurtling over the cliffs, actions that match those of Hitler's Gestapo. The behaviour of followers reflects the character of their leader. I am not surprised that Amaziah soon turned to worshipping pagan gods.

Lord, please help me to scrutinize my actions and my motives, that I may be wholehearted for you.

RG

Solid building

Uzziah built towers in Jerusalem at the Corner Gate, at the Valley Gate, and at the Angle, and fortified them. He built towers in the wilderness and hewed out many cisterns, for he had large herds, both in the Shephelah (i.e. foothills) and in the plain.

Uzziah appears to deserve an A* in all areas of his life and leadership—in his spirituality and his obedience to God (vv. 4, 5); in the effectiveness of his military campaigns (vv. 6–8); in his urban building and defences (v. 9); in his agricultural development (v. 10); in the training and equipment of his army (vv. 11–15). Every sphere of his life appears to be in good order. But did you notice that his home and family life are not mentioned? They were of little interest to the writer of Chronicles—and maybe of little interest to a workaholic, methodical king. It is sad when parents (yes, mothers as well as fathers) are so taken up with the demands of their work that they neglect the joys and responsibilities of the most important job in the world—parenting.

Parenting, too, is about building—building lives. Children's lives need good foundations and good nurturing—food, love, mental stimulus, moral and ethical training, social skills. Above all, they need the foundation of which Jesus spoke: 'I will show you what someone is like who comes to me, hears my words, and acts on them' (Luke 6:47). We know his illustration; the house built on rock withstood the storms, but the house built on sand collapsed as soon as the rain came and the river burst. Modern culture largely disregards Jesus' words and standards. Its 'rain and storms' are powerful. How important it is that we build solidly for our children. But we cannot put those foundations in place for our children if we ourselves do not hear, and obey, God's teaching.

Whether or not you have children of your own, pray for wisdom and skill for Christian parents and teachers. Make a list of children you know, for whose spiritual—and general—development you want to pray regularly.

RG

Pride and a fall

*But after Uzziah became powerful, his pride led to his downfall…
He had leprosy until the day he died. He lived in a separate house
—leprous, and excluded from the temple of the Lord. Jotham his
son had charge of the palace and governed the people of the land.*

'But'—a small word, but a significant one, that in verse 16 marks a
turning point in Uzziah's life. This successful king had reached a
pinnacle. His accomplishments and his power went to his head, and
thereafter he was on a steep and slippery slope.

Step 1   The decline started when he thought he had the right to
usurp the priest's job, the privilege of burning incense in the
temple.

Step 2   When confronted by Azariah and 80 other priests he had the
opportunity for humble apology. But he wasn't used to being
challenged, nor to apologizing. Instead he became furious.
Mercifully he hit out with words, not with the hot, heavy
censer.

Step 3   Leprosy broke out on his forehead. While not the leprosy of
modern days, it was a viciously contagious skin disease.

Step 4   He was hastily, and permanently, removed from the temple.

Step 5   He lived alone, under house arrest, for the rest of his life.

Step 6   He had to relinquish all power, while his son Jotham took
over the reins of government as prince regent.

Step 7   In his death he was even excluded from the royal burial
ground.

---

*It was a sad end for a mighty king. But beware! It is not easy to
be successful yet remain humble. Read Paul's well-known words in
1 Corinthians chapter 13: 'Love does not envy, it does not boast, it is
not proud.' The solidity, the ballast of love means that we neither have
to say—or think—'I'm better than you are' nor 'I wish I had what
you've got.' Rather we can say, 'Thank you, God, that you have made
me as I am. Please help me to use my gifts and my position in a way
that pleases you.'*

RG

Consistency

Jotham grew powerful because he walked steadfastly before the Lord his God.

Jotham was still a young man when he became king. It would be easy to overlook this short chapter given to his reign of 16 years, marked neither by highlights nor by low points. He continued Uzziah's work, building both in Jerusalem and in the countryside. He ran a successful military campaign against the Ammonites. He obeyed God, though, sadly, he did not stamp out pagan worship. Verse 2, 'he did not enter the temple' is not, of course, saying that he stayed away from temple worship; it refers to his father's audacity in burning incense there.

What marks Jotham out as special is that one short verse. He 'grew powerful because he walked steadfastly before the Lord his God'. The steadiness of his obedience to the Lord is remarkable. He did not move from mountain peak to crevasse, as many of us do. Rather he lived consistently on a high plateau, as it were. We are not told in what ways that 'steadfast walk' was expressed, but I guess that regularity in worship, obedience to God and consistency of character were all part of it—none of Uzziah's explosive anger. Could it be said of you that you 'walk steadfastly before the Lord'? Use this checklist.

- Do you worship regularly with other Christians?
- Do you read your Bible and pray each day?
- Do you arrive punctually for work?
- Are you honest and transparent in your dealings with people?
- Do you easily lose your temper?
- How patient are you in a traffic jam?
- Do you complain when things trouble you?
- Do you apologize for your mistakes?
- Do you inconvenience yourself to help other people?
- Do you persevere when a task gets difficult?
- How do you express compassion for the needy?

What other marks are there in your life of your consistent—or inconsistent—walk with God?

Lord, please help me to be steadier in my walk with you.

RG

Start as you mean to go on

In the first month of the first year of his reign, [Hezekiah]
opened the doors of the temple of the Lord and repaired them.
He brought in the priests and the Levites... and said...
'Consecrate yourselves now, and consecrate the temple of the
Lord. Remove all defilement from the sanctuary.'

Ahaz, Jotham's son, was an unmitigated disaster. With his Baal worship, his sons sent through the fire, his unholy alliances—he went
from one desperate, unsuccessful measure to another. He, too, was
not buried with his ancestors. We omit chapter 28; read this
unsavoury tale if you want to! Hezekiah his son, who succeeded him,
started reforms immediately. 'In the first month of the first year',
I like that. No beating about the bush for Hezekiah! Sometimes, of
course, a new leader is wise to take time in making changes, to win
trust before changing the status quo. But here was total ungodliness.
Hezekiah had no doubt about what needed to be done, and he
wasted no time in enlisting the support of the priests and Levites. He
challenged them to reconsecrate themselves to God and to clean out
the temple. They set to enthusiastically (vv. 15–19).

What does this say to us, 2500 years later? Perhaps you are starting a new job or living among new neighbours. Don't be afraid to let
your Christian standards show, remembering that this is your
lifestyle, not one that you are aggressively foisting on others. Maybe
you are wondering whether your children are old enough for Bible
story and bedtime prayers. It is never too early to start. Praying over
them in their cots leads naturally to praying with them. As soon as
they enjoy stories, a 'special book' for bedtime can be introduced.
Has some bad habit sneaked into your life? Make yourself account-
able to a trusted friend, as well as promising God to reform. Start,
and restart, as you mean to go on.

Lord, you know where I need a fresh start. Please help me to start,
and continue, in your way.

                                                              RG

Is your God real?

This is what Sennacherib king of Assyria says: On what are you
basing your confidence?… Who of all the gods of these nations
that my father destroyed has been able to save his people from me?
How then can your god deliver you from my hand?

'On what are you basing your confidence?' That is a good question
for any of us, at any time. It is particularly appropriate in a difficult situation. And the people of Jerusalem were indeed in a difficult
situation, under threat from the invading Assyrian forces. King
Sennacherib sent his officers from 25 miles away, where they were
besieging the fortified city of Lachish. They brought a letter; they
shouted outside the city walls; they did all they could to instil doubts
in the minds of the citizens of Jerusalem. 'Don't let Hezekiah mislead
you! Why do you think your God is better than any other god?'

That is another good question for us to consider. Christianity used
to be unchallenged in our society, but now it is different. We need to
be sure why we believe that our God is the true God. Jesus had no
doubt about himself: 'No one comes to the Father except through
me' (John 14:6). Peter had no doubt: 'There is no other name under
heaven given to men by which we must be saved' (Acts 4:12). Jesus
Christ stands head and shoulders above any other religious leader.
He is unique.

We could do worse than to learn by heart Hezekiah's words of
encouragement to his leaders before the Assyrian messengers
arrived: 'Be strong and courageous. Do not be afraid or discouraged
because of the king of Assyria and the vast army with him, for there
is a greater power with us than with him. With him is only the arm
of flesh, but with us is the Lord our God to help us and to fight our
battles' (32:7, 8).

Lord, please help me to be 100 per cent sure of you.

RG

A transformed life

*While he [Manasseh] was in distress he entreated the
favour of the Lord his God and humbled himself greatly
before the God of his ancestors. He prayed to him, and
God received his entreaty, heard his plea, and restored him
again to Jerusalem and to his kingdom.*

If you ever want evidence that an evil person can be changed, read
about Hezekiah's son Manasseh. He was a nasty piece of work! He
not only worshipped the sun, moon and stars, but he built Baal
altars in the temple precincts and erected an idol in the temple
itself. He went deep into witchcraft and even sacrificed his son in
the fire. His people followed his lead, 'so that they did more evil
than the nations whom the Lord had destroyed before the people of
Israel' (v. 9). Leadership can be for good or for evil.

God spoke to Manasseh and to the people, probably through a
prophet. But they refused to listen. (Have you ever ignored God
speaking to you through the words of a faithful friend?) Manasseh
was taken prisoner by the Assyrians, shackled and deported to
Babylon. In distress, he humbled himself and prayed. Plea, entreaty;
those words show a depth of repentance in his earnest prayer. God
heard him, and Manasseh was restored to his kingdom.

What is your reaction? Perhaps it is, 'But he was vile! He didn't
deserve that!' No, he didn't. But none of us deserve God's grace—
his free, unmerited favour and forgiveness. We may not have sunk
to Manasseh's abysmal standards, but I guess we all have skeletons
in our cupboards of which we are ashamed. And in his generosity
God says, 'Repent; change your ways, and I will do new things
for you.'

A few years ago Jonathan Aitken was one of the most despised of
our politicians, convicted of perjury, bankrupted and imprisoned.
I know Jonathan now, and I see a man transformed from pride and
perjury to gracious humility, in a life dedicated to Jesus Christ.

---

*Lord, thank you for your grace that changes lives, that changes even
me.*

RG

God's book

*He read in their hearing all the words of the book of
the covenant that had been found in the house of the Lord.
The king stood in his place and made a covenant before
the Lord, to follow the Lord, keeping his commandments...
with all his heart and all his soul.*

It was a great find! Josiah, Manasseh's grandson, was only a child
when he became king, and barely out of his teens when he started
reforms, destroying the pagan altars and idols that were again in use.
Then he collected money for the restoration of the temple, which
had fallen into disrepair. Verses 10–13 give us a picture of a busy,
well-ordered building site.

Then came the discovery of the book of the law of the Lord—
scrolls of the first five books of the Bible. When he first heard it
read, Josiah was dismayed, as he realized how disobedient the nation
had been. 'Great is the Lord's anger that is poured out on us because
our fathers have not kept the word of the Lord' (v. 21 NIV).

The strength of his reaction shows up my apathy. All round me
live people who ignore God and disregard his standards—and I take
it for granted. I am sad when I see churchpeople flouting God's laws,
but I cannot pretend to share Josiah's dismay. He was aware how
much God minds our disobedience, an awareness reinforced by the
message that came back from the prophetess Huldah, 'This is what
the Lord says: I am going to bring disaster upon this place and its
people... because they have forsaken me' (vv. 24, 25 NIV). God's
judgment was going to fall, through Judah's defeat and deportation
at the hands of the Assyrians. And I believe that God's judgment
(an unfashionable word!) will fall on the disobedience of our generation, though I don't know how or when.

---

*Josiah's response was a fresh commitment to God and his commands.
And I pray that as we read the Bible it may be a living, vital book that
leads each of us to renewed love and obedience to Jesus.*

RG

Too late!

The Lord... sent persistently to them by his messengers, because he had compassion on his people and on his dwelling-place; but they kept mocking the messengers of God, despising his words, and scoffing at his prophets until the wrath of the Lord against his people became so great that there was no remedy.

A royal dynasty that started four centuries earlier with David ended in total corruption. One family member succeeded another as king. Jehoahaz was deposed and taken to Egypt. Jehoiakim, who did unspecified 'detestable things' in his reign, was attacked by King Nebuchadnezzar and taken in shackles to Babylon. Jehoiachim followed three months later. Zedekiah reigned for 11 years. He refused to listen to the prophet Jeremiah; he refused to turn back to the Lord, and under him the people indulged increasingly in pagan practices. It is a sorry tale.

How would you expect God to act? He did not ignore his people, but they ignored him. I have in my mind an image of God, filled with compassion and grief, stretching out his arms towards his people, pleading with them, while they worship at an altar dedicated to Baal. Because in the Bible the prophets, his messengers, are separated from the historical books it is easy to forget that they were contemporary. Isaiah, Jeremiah, Amos, Hosea, Micah and Zephaniah all spell it out in their opening verses.

We like to focus on God's love, gentleness and power. But he is also utterly pure and holy, as Habakkuk, another contemporary prophet, expressed it: 'Your eyes are too pure to behold evil' (Habakkuk 1:13). God never loses control; but like parents whose patience runs out against a wilful child, his holy wrath is unleashed against unholy people. The writer of 2 Chronicles sees the hand of God in judgment behind the deportation of the people of Judah to Babylon. Jeremiah prophesied that this would happen—and also that they would return from captivity after 70 years. God's love shows through, even in the midst of his wrath.

How does your concept of God's character affect the way you live?

RG

Changed into his likeness

And all of us, with unveiled faces, seeing the glory of the Lord as though reflected in a mirror, are being transformed into the same image from one degree of glory to another: for this comes from the Lord, the Spirit.

The world we live in is very image-conscious—houses and gardens, as well as people, have television makeovers, providing a different style, a different image. And next month we can change it again! Sometimes this kind of process is simply fun, but it can become so important to have the right look that people spend more time and money than they can afford on searching for the right image. It actually does matter what kind of first impressions we make on the outside. But what about the inside? We can usually see where others need a character makeover! But what are we like deep down? Where do we need to change?

Paul tells the Christians of Corinth that anyone who decides to follow Jesus as their Lord is from that moment being changed into the likeness of Jesus by the Spirit. One day each Christian will stand before God 'conformed to the image of his Son, that he [Jesus] might be the firstborn within a large family' (Romans 8:29).

But we have a part to play in this transformation and Paul wrote about this lifelong struggle to become like Jesus, comparing it to the hard training of the soldier or the athlete. So what can we do to become more like Jesus? How can we learn to answer the question, 'What would Jesus do?' in any situation? One answer is that we can look at what he did and learn from him. Over the next two weeks we will look at some of the stories of Jesus, see how he acted, the qualities he revealed, and ask ourselves whether there is an example to follow.

Lord, thank you for giving me your Spirit to work your transforming power in my life. Help me to do my part to make me more like Jesus.
MK

Jesus—God and man

So he came to a town in Samaria called Sychar... Jacob's well was there, and Jesus, tired as he was from the journey, sat down by the well. It was about the sixth hour (noon).

In the beginning was the Word, and the Word was with God, and the Word was God. He was with God in the beginning. Through him all things were made... And the Word became flesh and lived for a while among us.

Jesus, tired, sits down on the edge of a well in the midday heat. He does something very ordinary, very human. We all know what it feels like to be tired, hot and thirsty. In the Gospel accounts we catch glimpses of him doing other ordinary things, going to a wedding, sitting down to supper with friends, sleeping at the bottom of a boat. He was a human being. He was like us.

John began his Gospel with the powerful words quoted in our text today, telling us that Jesus is God, the Lord and creator of the universe. How then *can* we be like him? There is such an enormous gulf between these two views of Jesus, reported by someone who lived and worked with him closely. John knew Jesus as a man and a friend, but he knew he was God.

This is the heart of the Christian faith. We know that in some way beyond our understanding he is both. Someone once said that if he had simply been a man he could not have saved us, but if he had not been a man he could not have died for us. There is powerful assurance in knowing that our Lord has not only divine power and sovereignty, but also human experience and understanding. So we can seek to imitate him in the way he lived on earth, knowing that he is with us by his Spirit to help us.

Read John 1:1–14 and worship him as Lord and Saviour, who has carried the marks of his humanity right up to the throne of heaven.

MK

Learning with Jesus

When the apostles returned, they reported to Jesus what they had
done. Then he took them with him and they withdrew...

I remember making pastry with a four-year-old, an interesting lesson
in patience. Knowing that pastry should not be handled too much
was not the best tip for someone who enjoyed the roly-poly part
more than any other. But now the four-year-old is an adult, making
pastry for her own family. We learn many of our skills by watching,
listening and sharing the experience with a teacher. Jesus was a
teacher and like the best teachers he 'took them with him'. Whether
a student teacher in a classroom, a student nurse on a ward, or an
engineering apprentice on the shop floor, most of us learn best by
watching someone else and then working beside them.

So the first story we look at is Luke's account of Jesus taking
loaves and fishes, a picnic for one, and using them to feed five
thousand. As we read this, we can use our imagination to be there
with Jesus and learn with the disciples how he does things. Then,
whether it's bringing up children, running a youth group, working
on a committee, or having responsibility for others at work, we can
begin to learn how to be this kind of teacher.

So how did Jesus do it? He listened to them as they told him what
they had been doing; he took them with him on his working journey; he suggested that they took action to deal with the problem of
the hungry crowd; and then when they were at a loss he gave them
a task they could do, organizing the crowd into groups; and then,
although the power, authority and the miracle were his, he got them
to distribute the food.

Help me, Lord, to be someone who has time to encourage and share
as I teach or train. Help me to give time for people to learn in their
own way. Give me the patience and love of a true teacher.

MK

Being generous

*Taking the five loaves and the two fish and looking up
to heaven, he gave thanks and broke them. Then he gave them to
the disciples to set before the people. They all ate and were
satisfied, and the disciples picked up twelve basketfuls of broken
pieces that were left over.*

Some years ago an anxious young woman at a station asked me for the fare to get home to her grandmother. I didn't know whether to believe her, nor did I have less than a £20 note. I hesitated and then gave it to her. Should I have given her anything? Should I have given much more than her fare? Now I know that I probably shouldn't, because this is a very common ploy to get money. I should have offered to buy her ticket! Generosity is not always easy. Even our regular charitable generosities are measured exactly, with CAF cheques and gift aid forms. No spontaneity and no space to say 'keep the change'!

Today we look again at this familiar story of the feeding of the five thousand, but this time focus on Jesus' generosity. We may not immediately notice just how generous Jesus was, that in his giving he goes further than necessary and ends up with too much! Six times, this event and a similar miracle are recorded and each time the writers record the amount of leftovers!

This overflowing generosity doesn't measure things grudgingly or sparingly, but gives with pleasure and perhaps with a sense of fun. It is the generosity of creation on a slightly smaller scale! This is generosity that does not count the pennies.

But the hidden factor in Jesus' generosity is his perfect relationship of trust with his heavenly father. If we trust God in our giving—whether money, hospitality or anything else—then we can be generous-minded and open-hearted, giving pleasure, as well as leaving baskets of leftovers.

---

*Help me to enjoy being generous with my money, my time and my life,
without counting, but with prayerful thought.*

MK

Being compassionate

When Jesus landed and saw a large crowd, he had compassion on them and healed their sick.

'I know you've had a hard day so I'll put the kids to bed.' Compassion, sympathy, understanding—how heart-warming it is when someone has compassion. From the simple things, like helping get luggage or children into a train, to the more demanding, like taking on the care of an increasingly handicapped friend.

At the beginning of Matthew's account of the feeding of the five thousand, Jesus looked at this large crowd, some sick, and all becoming hungry, having followed him to an isolated part of the lake shore, and had compassion on them. He understood their needs. So he acted. He healed the sick and then he fed them miraculously. He had compassion on them. That was the first step. He had the eyes and ears to see and hear what was happening to other people. The next step was that he had the heart to want to do something about it, and the third step, that he did all he could.

We do not have his clear vision of the needs of others, nor do we have his heart of compassion in such fullness. Nor can we work the same miracles, however much we may long to deal with the suffering that often wrings our hearts. But we can learn to be more aware of others and their needs, when driving, travelling, shopping, working, being with family and friends. It may not always need action, perhaps just a quick prayer for someone. Being aware of people and having a heart of compassion can change lives.

Being compassionate makes demands on us. We know that we sometimes simply cannot find the will to act. We would prefer to find a way out of responding to needs that are very demanding. Our compassion even for those we love can wear thin sometimes. Then we need to turn to him again, seeking his Spirit's power to transform us into being more like him.

Lord, help me to see the needs of others today.

MK

Welcoming children

Let the little children come to me, and do not hinder them, for the
kingdom of God belongs to such as these.

Of course, we all love children and especially babies. That's obvious.
But is it? There are many places and times in today's busy world
where children in general and babies in particular are out of place,
inappropriate, even embarrassing—in the office, on a rush-hour
train, in a seminar. More women are choosing not to have children
and some couples see children as simply a disruption of a comfortable lifestyle. They make a lot of noise, demand long-term attention
and restrict freedom.

There are a number of groups who are treated as inappropriate or
in the wrong place—mothers of small children often suffer from
embarrassed unspoken rebuke in public places. But the elderly and
the disabled can also be made to feel unwelcome, out of place or
embarrassing because they need extra consideration in a busy world.

Out of place? Absolutely not, said Jesus. They are to be encouraged: let the mothers bring them right into the centre of the group.
The disciples were, I hope, the ones really embarrassed as Jesus held
and blessed these babies and children.

But this wasn't just a rather touching and heart-warming inter-
lude. Jesus was still teaching, even as he held a child. The babies
were not only welcomed for their own sakes, but also to reinforce
the truth that unless we receive the kingdom of God like a child we
will never enter it. So we should perhaps look hard at the children
we know and meet; we should welcome them and begin to learn the
lessons that Jesus was teaching. No pretence? No artificiality? But
simplicity, innocent trust, lack of self-importance. Jesus welcomed
children. We should do the same—and learn from them.

Lord, help me to welcome children for your sake, and to learn from
them. Help me, too, to welcome into fellowship all those who are
pushed to the fringes as embarrassing or out of place.

MK

Having time for people

Then a man named Jairus, a ruler of the synagogue, came and fell at Jesus' feet, pleading with him to come to his house... As Jesus was on his way, the crowds almost crushed him. And a woman was there who had been subject to bleeding for twelve years...

How do you manage your time? This morning I drove half a mile to the dentist, because I hadn't the time to walk. The washing is still in the machine because I haven't had the time to get it out. I'm glad it's raining because I haven't the time to water the garden. I haven't time to stop.

So reading this chapter again I was struck by the way Jesus stopped and made time for those who needed him. How would I cope with the sudden need of a stranger that required me to stop where I was going, cancel what I was doing, and spend as much time as it takes to help them? I know that if this happened to me I would feel cornered, resentful that I could not keep to my crowded timetable for that day.

Jesus stops, listens to the anguished cry of Jairus, whose daughter is dying, and then on his way to Jairus' house, stops again for the women with the haemorrhage. He gives her his full attention, does all that is needed to restore her and heal her, and then moves on to give Jairus and his daughter his undivided attention.

I pray that God will use me, but in my busyness I do not always let him. Many of us need to ask ourselves where our priorities are. Is it more important that a child is washed, dressed and fed (in a hurry!) than played with, sung to, hugged? Is it more important that cheques are put in the bank, and the house tidied, than a lonely friend is invited in? This is not everyone's problem, but it is certainly mine. I need Jesus' help to start developing Jesus' priorities.

Lord, help me to get my priorities right today.

MK

Loving the unloved

A man with leprosy came and knelt before him and said, 'Lord, if you are willing, you can make me clean'. Jesus reached out his hand and touched the man.

People with leprosy were excluded from the social life of the community. This harsh exclusion was part of the Old Testament law that helped to limit the spread of contagious diseases. The woman with a twelve-year haemorrhage we read about yesterday would also have been excluded. That would mean that any one—family or friends— would be considered unclean if they were touched by her. Such people had to live away from others and were not allowed to attend synagogue or social events.

Jesus broke these laws; he 'ate with tax collectors and "sinners"'; he spent time with the socially excluded; he reached out his hand and touched the man with leprosy; he put his arm round those who were shunned. He broke social convention to meet the down-and-out, the disabled, and the beggars. He touched the dead body of Jairus' little girl, and a widow's only son, even though the dead, too, were 'unclean'. He healed and restored them so that they could go back into their communities to be included in the social life around them. He told them to go to the priests for the medical examination that would show they were healed and could go back to family and friends.

I once pushed a friend round our town in a wheelchair and I became aware that many people who knew us both spoke to me over his head. He was being excluded, although others did not realize they were doing it. Who is excluded from your circle of friends, from your church fellowship? Those with learning difficulties? Those with difficult personalities? Those housebound?

Lord, if I really want to follow you, then I have to follow you in this. Help me to be willing to move out of comfortable fellowship and to reach out to those on the edges, who are left out.

MK

Learning to pray

One of those days Jesus went to a mountainside to pray, and spent the night praying to God. When morning came, he called his disciples to him and chose twelve of them.

Jesus was about to decide on the twelve men who would be his closest disciples. So he went away to a quiet place and spent the night in prayer. This was a significant moment and much would depend on his choice. This night of deep, focused prayer matched the importance of the decision.

But we may wonder why Jesus needed to do this. He was one with his Father in ways that are beyond our understanding. Every moment of his life was focused dependence and communication with God. Only that moment on the cross when he touched the depths of separation would that communication falter. Yet he went out into the hills for a night of prayer.

Jesus shows us the importance of special times of prayer for important decisions. Most of us recognize this need and seek this kind of deep prayer for guidance and wisdom for big decisions. But the ongoing walk of daily prayer, talking to the Lord, can be the point of greatest struggle.

Prayer fits awkwardly into a busy life. The very word 'prayer' resonates with slowing down, sitting still, being alone, shutting our eyes. It is not about quick responses and one-line e-mails; it doesn't fit with crowded trains, demanding children, fussing colleagues. Prayer ends up swept into hasty getting-up and sleepy before-lights-out times.

But that is exactly what Jesus' life was like—full of crowds and clamour, endless demands, dusty roads and temporary homes. So maybe we should practise the presence of God as Jesus did—praying about each day as it happens, the decisions, the joys and disappointments, the individuals we meet, our work—quick prayers, short prayers, but a real attempt to communicate with the Lord in the middle of a busy world.

If we want to follow Jesus, then we really do need to follow him in this as well.

MK

Being a friend

Jesus took Peter, James and John with him and led them up a high mountain, where they were all alone. There he was transfigured before them.

The other day I investigated the website that aims to bring old school friends together. I looked at the names of some of the girls I knew once and was overwhelmed with memories. I have failed to keep up with any of them, even though, with one or two, the foundations for a lifetime's friendship were laid. Friendship is often a casualty of modern life, where mobility and busyness make the effort of keeping up difficult. The regrets come later.

Jesus seems to have had a wide circle of friends who travelled with him, with an inner core of the 12 disciples. Several times he singled out the three who were closest to him, Peter, James and John, and took them to be with him for special times. So they were there when his glory as the Son of God shone out, and when he prayed in anguish as he faced the cross (14:33).

As we look at his friendship with Peter in particular, we can see that Jesus had a far closer relationship with friends than he had with his family, who did not seem to have understood his ministry and were not followers until after the resurrection. 'Who are my mother and my brothers? Whoever does God's will is my brother and sister and mother', he says at one point (Mark 3:31–34). For the many who remain single and who are far from family, this can be an encouragement to build real friendships.

He was also committed to his friends, even when they failed him. He knew Peter would deny that he knew him when he was arrested. But at the first opportunity he restores and forgives Peter. Honesty, truthfulness and forgiveness are important in true friendship. So is encouragement and empowering. Jesus does not just forgive Peter but he trusts him with the leadership and pastoring of the new church.

Why not contact an old friend today?

MK

Learning humility

Then the devil took him to the holy city and had him stand on the highest point of the temple. 'If you are the Son of God, throw yourself down.'

Straight after Jesus had been baptized and had heard the voice of God affirming him as his Son, he was led into the desert to face temptation. Can this lonely spiritual battle teach us how to follow him?

The tempter begins twice with the words, 'If you are the Son of God'. He is suggesting that if Jesus has the authority and power to perform miracles, then he should do so and turn stones into bread, demonstrate that he is divine so that all can see, and enjoy being Lord over all the 'splendour' of this world.

Jesus does have power; he shows that many times—in healing, in quieting a storm, in breaking a loaf to feed thousands and in teaching with authority. But he does not use his power for himself; he does not make people believe in him by stunning them with a very visible show of power; he refuses to take a short cut to being the Lord of all. He knows that he has to take the humble servant route, through death to glory. He will not be tempted to use power to take the easy way.

Anyone who has any kind of power—bosses, parents, teachers, the rich, the influential—faces this kind of temptation. Even evangelists and preachers can use eloquence and atmosphere to overwhelm. We find it difficult when people don't seem to know who we are or talk to us as if we are not very important. We are greedy for status and appreciation. But not insisting on our rightful place at the banquet is a life-changing quality. Jesus chose not to grasp his rightful position, but gave up the glory of heaven to live on earth. Until we learn that this is the way, we will not understand the enormous gulf that Jesus bridged in the incarnation and on the cross.

Read Luke 14:7–11.

MK

Facing suffering

Going a little further, he fell with his face to the ground and prayed, 'My Father, if it is possible, may this cup be taken from me. Yet not as I will, but as you will.

Most of us at some time in our lives have to face suffering. And suffering comes in different forms. Jesus faced a cruel death, and shrank from it. He also endured betrayal, denial and abandonment by his friends, mob violence, the casual brutality of soldiers, false witnesses and injustice for political reasons.

All over the world, 'Please don't let this happen to me' rings out over and over again. When faced with the unfairness and injustice of much suffering, our cry is, 'Why?' There are often no satisfactory answers and human suffering can be a huge stumbling-block to faith in a God of love. But here in the Garden of Gethsemane, Jesus' anguished prayer for a way out and on the cross, his cry, 'Why, my God, have you left me alone?' is part of human suffering. Our Lord knows what it is like.

Jesus' death is the most important event in the history of the world. It is God's plan for salvation, his way of dealing with human sin and rebellion. But it also means that the Lord we serve walked through suffering and death to vindication and resurrection. He calls us to take up our cross *and* believe that we too will rise to be with him in glory.

Sometimes we bear the suffering of our own and others' sin, but often we do not know why suffering comes. Jesus shows us that suffering can be redemptive, turned to good, although not always and not easily. Suffering can teach us lessons about ourselves. It can give us better understanding of others. It can drive us to fight for a better world, to seek cures for disease and to fight injustice and hunger.

We have a Lord who knows what suffering means, and walks with us through the valley of the shadow of death.

MK

Learning to live with little?

Foxes have holes and birds of the air have nests, but the Son of Man has nowhere to lay his head.

We never hear of Jesus going to his own house; he stays with friends; he borrows a room in someone's house for his last meal; he tells a would-be disciple that he doesn't have a bed of his own.

There are other things he lacked. He never married. He never reached middle age. He seems not to have had any money, but a common purse, provided with funds by followers, for his and his disciples' needs. He had little privacy unless he went out at night into the hills. 'Do not store up for yourselves treasures on earth', he said, 'for where your treasure is, there your heart will be also.' He lived a full, perfect, wholly holy life without most of the things we take for granted.

If only I were married. If only I had a better job. If only I were healthy. If only I lived in a better place. We all live with longings that cannot be fulfilled, but can destroy our happiness and our peace with God, if we let them. Jesus shows us that it is possible to live a full and purposeful life, with rich friendships and a close relationship with God, with little earthly treasure.

The way we respond to 'handicaps'—to limitations on our lives —is more important for a full life, than the 'handicaps' themselves. If our hopes and dreams are only for material things, then we are bound for disappointment and regret. But true peace and true happiness depend on our relationship with Jesus, who said, 'In this world you will have trouble. But take heart! I have overcome the world' (John 16:33). Take heart and enjoy what we have, put aside anything that might lead us away from holiness and know that one day all the riches of his glory will be ours.

Read Romans 5:1–5.

MK

Breakfast with Jesus

*Early in the morning, Jesus stood on the shore, but the disciples
did not realize that it was Jesus… Jesus said to them, 'Come and
have breakfast.' None of the disciples dared ask him, 'Who are
you?' They knew it was the Lord.*

Oh, what a beautiful morning! Sunrise beside the lake, and Jesus
gets a small fire going so that the freshly caught fish can be grilled
for breakfast. The disciples stumble ashore and join him to eat. Here
is another very human moment, idyllic, peaceful and simple.

Only there is a difference. The relationship has changed. This is
the risen Christ. He died and was buried. They are certain of that,
but not yet fully sure of just who he is now. There must have been
amazement, disbelief and a huge growing joy ever since he came
back from the dead. How can anything go wrong again?

He cooks for them, cares for them and reassures them, particularly Peter. But soon he will leave them and they will never see him
again. There will be fear, persecution, martyrdom and exile, but
there will be the exhilaration of preaching the gospel in the Spirit's
power and seeing the Church grow and spread. It will all be worthwhile.

But for now, on this quiet morning round the fire, they realize
once and for all that he is indeed the promised Christ, risen from the
dead, but he is also still their friend, teacher and brother, who serves
them breakfast. There is no one else to follow, no other example to
copy. He is the only Lord, the only Saviour, our vision, our hope and
our example.

High king of heaven, when battle is done,
Grant heaven's joy to me, O bright heaven's sun,
Christ of my own heart, whatever befall,
Still be my vision, O ruler of all.

GAELIC, EIGHTH CENTURY, TRANSLATED BY ELEANOR HULL

MK

Light

God is light and in him there is no darkness at all... If we walk in the light... we have fellowship with one another, and the blood of Jesus his Son cleanses us from all sin.

This is the shortest day of the year, at least in the northern hemisphere. And the longest night. It can be pretty dreary. Dark and dreary. But Christmas is approaching, and lights are springing up and appearing everywhere. Bright lights. Coloured lights. Christmas tree lights. The lights shine in the darkness.

Does that remind you of anything? What about the beginning of John's Gospel. In the first chapter John states, 'The light shines in the darkness' (John 1:5). In chapter 3 he tells us that 'people loved darkness rather than light' (John 3:19). How strange! Why was that? John says, in the same verse, that it was 'because their deeds were evil'. Our passage today gives us the good news that 'the blood of Jesus... cleanses us from all sin'.

It is not only in Europe that lights are symbolic at this time of the year. Several years ago, when I was editor of the magazine of my multi-ethnic church in Geneva, I asked Sushila to share something about Christmas customs in her home country of India. This is what she wrote: 'Every Indian festival is associated with lights and fireworks. Add to that a star, a decorated pine branch, a cake, a manger scene, and you have an Indian Christmas. Three-dimensional stars are made with bamboo strips, covered with paper, a light fixed inside and hung on the front porch... It is a time when one sees more stars on land than in the sky, and that seems very right. The Bright and Morning Star did leave his heavenly home and came to dwell among men on that first Christmas'.

Jesus said, 'I am the light of the world. Whoever follows me will never walk in darkness but will have the light of life' (John 8:12). Let us walk in the light, rejoicing that our sins have been forgiven.

BA

A dark world

'*I am the light of the world.*'

In Australia's Red Centre, I had the privilege one night of observing the stars with an astronomer. Because we were in the desert, far away from the lights of any town, the stars shone even more brightly in the dark sky. Speaking of the light that was coming into the world, John writes in his Gospel that 'the darkness did not overcome it' (John 1:5).

'I am the light of the world'. Twice Jesus utters these words, in chapter 8 of John's Gospel, when he is teaching in the temple, and then in the following chapter, just before opening the eyes of the man born blind. He reveals to people their condition—spiritual blindness—and shows them the truth about themselves and about God. 'Everyone who commits sin is a slave to sin', he says (John 8:34). And he continues, 'If the Son makes you free, you will be free indeed'.

'I am the light of the world, whoever follows me will never walk in darkness, but will have the light of life' (John 8:12). What a wonderful promise! God, in his mercy, has called us 'out of darkness into his marvellous light' (1 Peter 2:9). What a cause for celebrating this Christmas!

As disciples of Christ, we too are the light of the world. Jesus tells us to let our 'light shine before others, so that they may see [our] good works and give glory to [our] Father in heaven' (Matthew 5:14–16).

Have you ever noticed the strong link between living in the light and loving one's brother? 'Anyone who claims to be in the light but hates his brother is still in the darkness. Whoever loves his brother lives in the light' (1 John 2:9, NIV).

Let us follow Jesus and 'have the light of life'. May we be lights in this dark world, not only at Christmas, but always, as we reflect Jesus Christ and as we show love to our brothers and sisters. And may God be glorified through us.

BA

Presents and partying

Let the same mind be in you that was in Christ Jesus.

'Christmas in Singapore is one of the most eagerly awaited festivals, celebrated by people of every colour and creed', wrote Kok Wah and Connie in our church magazine. 'Hotels and shopping centres will try to outdo one another with increasingly more spectacular Christmas displays. Commercialized? Definitely.'

Around the middle of November my sister in England wrote that she had just about finished her Christmas shopping at 'a wonderful new shopping centre, with beautiful fountains and water features and fabulous shops'. (She is a lot more organized than I am!). Yes, the American mall has crossed the Atlantic and is springing up everywhere in Europe.

Some would consider these architectural wonders to be symptomatic of our post-modern world, places where one can pick and choose, all things being equal in a pluralistic society. They have even been likened to shrines, the worship place of consumerism.

Whether we agree with such an appraisal or not, beware of falling into the trap of materialism. Let us resist the temptation to conform to the world's view of Christmas—just an excuse for presents and partying. And yet we want to celebrate the One who has given us the greatest gift of all—eternal life.

Daisy and Daniel share with us that in Southern Cameroon, 'Christmas food is abundant and varied, and the best that can be afforded for the entire year. As a rule also, it is never meant to be eaten alone but to be widely shared with those around. God's generosity to mankind is thus proclaimed and manifested in a simple and concrete way'. In Eritrea too, Regat tells us, 'It is a tradition for those who have to share with those who have not.'

If a brother or sister is naked and lacks daily food, and one of you says to them, 'Go in peace; keep warm and eat your fill,' and yet you do not supply their bodily needs, what is the good of that? (James 2:15, 16).

BA

To celebrate or not…

He will save his people from their sins.

My husband Derek was pastor of the Evangelical Baptist Church of Geneva until his retirement. Here is the essence of an article he wrote for the church magazine.

Christmas is coming—traditionally the season of peace and goodwill. But both of these qualities seem to be in pretty short supply. So how should we celebrate the festive season?

It seems to me that we need to get back to the spirit of the 'first' Christmas to remind ourselves of the circumstances in which the 'Word became flesh'. It wasn't a 'nice' world. King Herod's murderous and suspicious nature led him not only to perpetrate the slaughter of the 'innocents' in order to eliminate a potential rival to his throne, but also to murder most of his close relatives, for fear of treachery. Likewise, the Roman occupation of Israel was a brutal and cruel regime. It was the Romans who brought the most barbaric form of execution—crucifixion—to a 'fine art'.

That is the context in which our Lord was born: a world of oppression and violence, of fear and insecurity, where injustice reigned. And Jesus was subjected to the most shameful and ugly death ever devised. All that is bound up in this event that we now celebrate, often in an orgy of artificial and superficial goodwill and spurious generosity. Is our world any better than the one in which Christ was born?

The only hope for this blighted world is not just freedom from terrorism or any other form of human wickedness, but freedom from the ultimate cause of all evil, sin itself. And that, to use a well-worn cliché, will be possible only if we put Christ back into Christmas. As the angelic messenger said to Joseph, some 2000 years ago: 'You are to name him Jesus, for he will save his people from their sins' (Matthew 1:21). It's as simple as that.

So how will you celebrate Christmas this year?

BA

Tinsel and trappings

Rejoice with me... There will be more joy in heaven over one sinner who repents than over ninety-nine righteous persons who need no repentance.

Have you ever heard anyone say, 'I can't stand Christmas pudding, Christmas cake and even mince pies'? Well, I have. And the negative sentiments did not stop there. This incipient Scrooge also strongly objects to the inevitable extra expenditure of this season. And that is not all. He is also of the opinion that 'even the religious traditions associated with Christmas are often more sentimental than spiritual, or at least so perverted that midnight mass is frequently followed by a midnight merrymaking binge'. And he continues: 'Songs like "Rudolph the red-nosed reindeer" and "I'm dreaming of a white Christmas" now make me cringe when I hear them.'

But surely he cannot object to Christmas carols! Don't you believe it: 'The problem is that even though some carols beautifully point beyond the birth to the cross, too often we celebrate the Babe of Bethlehem to the detriment of the Christ of Calvary. After all, everyone loves a baby, helpless, dependent, fragile. But who really likes to come face to face with a thorn-crowned King of kings?'

He concludes: 'Nevertheless, in spite of my grouses and grumbles, I will be celebrating Christmas this year, for somehow, somewhere, someone will find the real joy of Christmas behind the tinsel and toys and trappings. And therefore, in line with the gospel example of rejoicing over the finding of one lost sheep, I wish you a very happy Christmas'.

Who is this killjoy, anyway? I hate to confess that the above sentiments have all been expressed by my dearly beloved husband! He assures me, though, that he does like roast turkey with all the trimmings!

May we get beyond the trimmings to the heart of the good news this Christmas, the good news of salvation in Jesus, the Good Shepherd who laid down his life for the sheep.

BA

Christmas isn't Christmas...

And the Word became flesh and lived among us...
No one has ever seen God. It is God the only Son...
who has made him known.

As I have been reflecting on these notes, my mind has gone back to Zambia, the country of my childhood. I remember how we used to celebrate Christmas there in Lusaka. My memories are made up of a strange mixture of British colonialism and African customs. After all, Christmas isn't Christmas if one doesn't have turkey and stuffing and Christmas pudding, and snow on the Christmas cards... in the sweltering heat of Central Africa! I still remember the shivers up my spine and the thrills of fear and delight as native warriors, with masks and painted faces, leaped about and danced in our drive, brandishing their spears on Christmas Day.

Apollo, brought up in Argentina, remembers a Christmas celebration in his church when 'it was so hot that we had to take doors and windows away in order to have better air flow! One year we went carolling afterwards. It lasted till three o'clock in the morning and we only wore T-shirts and shorts!'

Amanda, who comes from Queensland, Australia, remembers 'one Christmas Day when temperatures reached a scorching 40 degrees... Christmas Day for most Australians is very relaxed, spent with family and relatives, sharing lunch together, often at the beach or by the pool. Traditional roast turkey with all the trimmings and pudding do not really mix well with the hot weather (although there are those who insist and then suffer afterwards). Many Australians have cold meats, salads and fruit, or sometimes a barbecue or picnic to celebrate Christmas Day. I feel sad that for all those people who treat Christmas as just another good reason to have a holiday. They do not want to know about the true meaning of Christmas.'

Wherever Christmas is kept, whatever traditions we are used to, Christmas isn't really Christmas if we do not celebrate the Word made flesh, God become man in the person of Jesus Christ.

BA

Christmas in other lands

Christ is proclaimed in every way... and in that I rejoice.

Some of the most enriching aspects of a multi-cultural church concern Christmas traditions. On Christmas Day, in our church in Geneva, we would have a short family service at which participants would wish the rest of the congregation 'Happy Christmas' in their own language.

In most places, Christmas is a family time. Sharing about customs in Sri Lanka, Nimal explains that 'at Christmas time, when we gathered in our grandfather's village, we spilled over into each other's houses'. In Nigeria, Abiodun tells us that 'the social aspect consists of sumptuous meals with family, relations and friends'.

It seems as if there is an emphasis on feasting in most traditions. In Jamaica, according to Philip, 'some of the specialities include curried goat, roast pork, Jamaican Christmas cake, and sorrel—a drink made from hibiscus'. Also, in many places people share with those who are less fortunate. In cities in Sri Lanka 'the church community makes a special effort to help families in need,' explains Nimal.

Clothes are not a negligible part of the festivities, either! In the Philippines 'the men are dressed in their traditional Barong shirts, a finely embroidered material woven out of pineapple fibres', says Cecilia. And in Nigeria, Abiodun points out that 'this is the time when the streets in the residential areas look colourful, not with flowers and garlands but with happy people, brightly dressed for parties, visits to friends and relations, and street parades'.

The culmination of all this activity and excitement is, in most cases, the church services. Sushila tells us that in India 'the first service normally begins before dawn'. In Haiti, where, as in many other countries, Christmas is celebrated on the evening of 24 December, Alta recounts that 'believers share experiences and testify to the love of God... These meetings... bring reconciliation with God and fellow men, a great source of blessing and renewal'.

For God so loved the world that he gave his only Son, so that everyone who believes in him may not perish but may have eternal life (John 3:16).

BA

128

2 Corinthians 5:17–21 (NRSV)

Reconciliation

If anyone is in Christ, there is a new creation: everything old has passed away; see, everything has become new! All this is from God, who reconciled us to himself through Christ, and has given us the ministry of reconciliation; that is, in Christ God was reconciling the world to himself… Be reconciled to God.

Throughout the worst of the war, John and Nancy, with their two children, stayed in Lebanon, where God had called them to reach young people with the gospel. As he avoided snipers on the streets of Beirut, John firmly believed that he and his family were safer there, in the centre of God's will, than they would have been in any other place.

It seems as if never before in the history of the world has there been greater need of the message of Christmas, a message of reconciliation, that 'Peace among men' (Luke 2:14 RSV) proclaimed by the heavenly host on the night of our Saviour's birth.

As we prepare to enter a new year, nation is at war with nation; civil war is rife in certain countries; families are divided and homes are broken; people are troubled, afraid to go out, afraid of the future. International and intergovernmental humanitarian organizations are working for world peace. Many are saying, as in the time of Jeremiah, '"Peace, peace", when there is no peace' (Jeremiah 6:14).

Throughout the ages, efforts to change society have failed. It is our hearts that must change first, hearts that Jeremiah qualifies as 'deceitful above all things, and desperately wicked' (Jeremiah 17:9 AV). Before nation is reconciled to nation, before civil wars cease, before broken relationships are mended, we must be reconciled to God.

Have you been reconciled to God through Christ? May we be faithful in exercising this 'ministry of reconciliation' that has been entrusted to us, and so be instrumental in bringing about 'peace among men' this Christmas.

BA

Luke 2:8–20 (NRSV)

Great joy!

I am bringing you good news of great joy for all the people.

The world was in darkness at the time of Jesus' birth. True, the Stoics, the Epicureans and the mystery religions attempted in different ways to meet people's fundamental needs. And all failed. A spirit of gloom and pessimism had settled over the human race.

It is into this darkness that the light shone! 'The light shines in the darkness' exclaimed John (John 1:5). It is to this gloomy, pessimistic world that 'good news of great joy' is announced! What exactly is this momentous news? It is the announcement of the birth of a Saviour. And what the pagan gods, the Stoics, the Epicureans and the mystery religions were not able to do, Jesus Christ did. He saved the people from their sins and gave them new life.

Shortly before going to the cross, Jesus said to his disciples, 'I have said these things to you so that my joy may be in you, and that your joy may be complete' (John 15:11). If we refer to the preceding verses, we discover what it was that Jesus had told them. He was speaking to them of his fellowship with the Father. 'As the Father has loved me, so I have loved you; abide in my love. If you keep my commandments, you will abide in my love, just as I have kept my Father's commandments and abide in his love' (John 15:9, 10). Then comes the verse about joy. The source of Jesus' joy was his fellowship with the Father, expressed through love and obedience. How then can we know the fullness of joy that he promises to his followers? Surely it is no different for us—our joy too depends on our love for God and our obedience to him.

Thank you Lord for the 'news of great joy'. Thank you for being my Saviour. Thank you for forgiving my sins so that I can enjoy fellowship with you. I love you, Lord. Help me to obey you.

BA

Life!

I came that they may have life, and have it abundantly.

In Europe for his studies, Amjad has become a believer in Jesus Christ and has been baptized. He will shortly return to his country of Pakistan, where his life could be in danger, as he will be a lone Christian in a Muslim society.

Persecution, war and strife among nations, and natural disasters have engendered death, famine, disease and homelessness—not to mention hopelessness. We have all heard the horrifying figures of those who have been wiped out and of those who are dying of hunger and cold. Figures? Rather, people! Each figure representing a person made in the image of God and for whom the Saviour came into the world.

'Vanity of vanities! All is vanity', exclaims the preacher (Ecclesiastes 1:2). Or, in a more modern translation, 'Nothing is worthwhile; everything is futile' (LB). But is this world of futility and meaninglessness all there is to life? No, certainly not! That is the whole point of Christmas! That is the whole point of the incarnation.

God stepped in. God, in the person of his Son Jesus Christ, became human and lived among us and suffered as we do, suffered as 'they' do in all the war-torn countries of the world and in places where natural disasters have claimed the lives of many and left others homeless. And he did not just suffer *with* us; he suffered *for* us. He suffered for us when he took upon himself that which is the cause of all human suffering—sin. That sin—humanity's sin, your sin, my sin—nailed him to the cross.

But the story does not end there. He rose from the dead, victorious over sin. And, in him, we can have that same victory. He stepped into this futile, meaningless existence to bring life. Real life. Abundant life. Eternal life.

Let us proclaim the message of eternal life and salvation this Christmastime in such a way that it will bring hope to the hopeless and new life to those who are dead in trespasses and sins.

BA

Walking in the dark

Let him who walks in the dark, who has no light, trust in the name of the Lord and rely on his God.

On the threshold of a new year, we look again at the theme of darkness and light. Do you feel as if you are walking in the dark? The circumstances of life have plunged you into a seemingly endless tunnel. You are depressed, maybe in despair. You are stepping into the new year without hope. You see no way out of your situation, no glimmer of light.

Listen to this exhortation: 'Let him who walks in the dark, who has no light, trust in the name of the Lord and rely on his God'. Notice the first verb. The verb 'to walk' indicates that life is not static. We are moving on. In order to see our way, we need light. God has provided us with that light. The psalmist declares, 'Your word is a lamp to my feet and a light for my path' (Psalm 119:105). If the road lies dark before us, let us open up the word of God, which sheds light upon our path.

The prophet encourages us to 'trust in the name of the Lord'. Even if the way seems dark, the Lord knows the way. He has lived this life on earth with all its suffering and anguish and pain, and he is with us in our difficulties. 'I will never leave you or forsake you' (Hebrews 13:5, NRSV) is his promise to us. Not only does he *know* the way, but he *is* the way (John 14:6). And has he not said, 'I am the light of the world, whoever follows me will never walk in darkness' (John 8:12)?

The possessive adjective 'his' towards the end of this verse indicates a relationship. Have you entered into a personal relationship with God through Jesus? If so, you can step into 2004 trusting him, relying on him, following the one who is the way, the truth, the life and the light.
BA

DAY
BY
DAY
WITH
GOD

MAGAZINE SECTION

Famous for fifteen minutes: the cult of celebrity

Fiona Barnard

On my birthday this year, a friend presented me with a wrapped-up copy of *Hello* magazine. 'I know how much you like *Hello*,' she said, 'so this is the first of a year's subscription for you.' I was staggered. I think it is the first time that I have pleaded with anyone to take a present back. 'But it's too much!' I kept saying. 'I can't take it. How about just a month's supply instead?' But alas, it was too late, and now, three months later, I can't help but get excited every Tuesday evening at the prospect of the magazine's arrival with the next morning's post.

Yet there is a problem: am I alone in feeling simultaneously drawn to the whole celebrity culture and at the same time repulsed by it? Am I the only Christian watching chat shows where stars are flattered, or TV programmes where a famous person condescends to live 'with ordinary people' for a couple of nights? Did any other *Day by Day with God* readers find themselves hooked on *Big Brother* or *Survivor* despite all good intentions to do something much more useful?

People

It has been said that a 'celebrity is a person who is known for his well-knownness' but despite recognizing the shallowness, the frivolity and the escapism of other people's fairytales and misery, I have to admit a certain fascination. At root, I suppose I am interested in people. I am curious to know what others think and experience, how it feels to be a toilet cleaner, a mother of six, a Chinese undergraduate, a three-legged flautist, and so on. (Well, that's my excuse...)

People buy into the cult of celebrity for different reasons. Some need heroes and heroines; they want people who will model their dreams for them, and perhaps offer guidance in the way they might live. Others like to put individuals on pedestals and then pull them down, content to show that they are really 'the same as us' after all. Many are lonely, and sadly may know more about the stars than they do about family or neighbours or friends; intimacy at a distance doesn't carry the same cost or demands.

What would Jesus say to all this? Would he go on *Parkinson* or let Ruby Wax visit his home? Would he watch soaps, read *OK* or vote someone out of the *Big Brother* house?

Exclusive

Jesus' words and deeds certainly made him a celebrity of sorts. Even without the tabloids, news about him spread far and wide. And so it is that Jesus' conversation with his disciples at Caesarea Philippi can be called a watershed in his story, for it revealed to his closest friends his startling personal mission statement. Having listened to what the popular 'press' was calling him, and having heard Peter's confession, 'You are the Christ/Messiah' (Mark 8:29), Jesus had a few surprises in store. Away from the crowds, he gave his very own 'exclusive' on just who he was, and on how he saw his life as part of God's greater plan. Today, his words reach across 2,000 years to challenge our celebrity-mad culture. He told them that, humanly speaking, the future was *not* 'bright' and that he would be viewed by many as a failure, for he was going to suffer and die. There was a further bombshell: Jesus stated that those who wished to follow him must tread the same path: 'If any want to become my followers, let them deny themselves and take up their cross and follow me. For those who want to save their life will lose it, and those who lose their life for my sake, and for the sake of the gospel, will save it' (Mark 8:34–35, NRSV).

The celebrity culture declares, 'Life is a ladder you climb. Use your money, looks, relationships, power and influence to get to the top.' Jesus says, 'If you want to be my disciple, the way up is down. You have to bend down and carry a cross.' The celebrity culture shouts, 'Life is about finding yourself. Take care of number one!' Jesus says, 'If you want to follow me, the way to find yourself is to lose yourself, to deny yourself.' The celebrity culture advises, 'Live for today: eat, drink and be merry, for tomorrow you may die of over-indulgence, a broken heart or something worse.' Jesus says, 'If you lose your life for my sake, you will save it. To lose is to win; to die is to live.' The celebrity PR people assert, 'Image is everything.' Jesus says, 'Following me is everything.'

Challenges

Jesus' values are radically counter-cultural. They challenge and reverse our common human assumptions. It's a wonder he has ever got anyone to follow him—unless, of course, he is right about the nature of life and living it.

Perhaps in their more sober moments, even those at the very centre of the circus might testify to his wisdom. For even the celebrity articles themselves carry stories of the distress that fame and fortune can bring. 'I was so big as an artist,' recalled Elton John in an interview recently, 'that I had no life.' Wealth and popularity are no protection against illness and broken relationships, isolation and fear, a sense of emptiness and worthlessness. Some time ago, I read an article about a TV personality who, finding herself single again, had managed to lose several stone in weight, and yet admitted, 'I'm worried about everything. I feel myself in a really difficult, lonely, frightening situation.' The picture of the smiling clown with the tear in his eye is an uncomfortable metaphor.

What, then, is the attraction of the celebrity culture? The successful are so often obviously just as flawed and needy as anyone. Indeed, we hear of some who need to read the tabloids to know who they are: their sense of worth is at the mercy of journalists and a fickle reading public. So it is a crazy to measure ourselves against those who are deemed to be the achievers, for it appears that they, too, often struggle in the area of self-esteem.

Special

How do I, ignored by the paparazzi and media, forgotten by old teachers and neighbours, and unnoticed in a crowd, measure my sense of worth? I am special, not because I am beautiful but because God made me. I am special, not because I am talented but because the Father loves me. I am special, not because I am rich but because Jesus died for me. I am special, not because I'm popular but because, as a Christian, God's Spirit actually lives in me. My value lies in the fact that God has stopped at nothing so that I can be his. And when

I allow the wonder of this fact to sink in, what else can I do but give myself back to him and to others in service?

I have heard it said many times, 'You must love yourself first, so that you can then love your neighbour.' I don't agree. The irony is that the more we try to love ourselves, the less we seem able to do it. That is why Jesus' words are so profound and so powerful. It is as we lose ourselves that we find ourselves. It is as we forget ourselves that we are liberated from the slavery to peer pressure and status seeking. It is as we deny our self-centred, self-preoccupied urges and desires for the sake of Jesus that we find true and lasting happiness and satisfaction.

Jesus' version of *Hello* isn't just surface gloss. It is full of real people whose teeth are crooked and whose hair sticks out in all the wrong places. They are eloquent, illiterate, well-known, living in the back of beyond, optimistic, melancholic, outgoing, shy and thousands of variations in between. Yet these things are not important to the heavenly interviewer and reporter. It is substance that counts. In different ways and situations, these followers of Jesus have discounted worldly standards and rewards for love of their Master. Often at great personal cost, they have cared for the sick; they have gossiped the gospel; they have fought injustice; they have loved the unlovely. These are God's celebrities, and I want to be among them.

Fiona Barnard lives in Scotland. As staff member of Friends International, her principal work is among international students and researchers, and encouraging local Christians to reach out in friendship to those temporarily far from home.

Perfectly piped pavlovas

Sue Morton

Christmas! So much to do, so little time in which to do it. We spend time rushing round in ever-decreasing circles and, when the big day finally arrives, do we enjoy it? Or do we sit there feeling exhausted, wondering if we put too much salt on the potatoes, or too many raisins in the Christmas pudding?

I've often wondered how Martha would have coped with Christmas. We read in Luke 10:40, 'Martha was distracted by all the preparations that had to be made. She came to (Jesus) and asked, 'Lord, don't you care that my sister has left me to do all the work by myself? Tell her to help me!' I'm sure we've all felt like this at some point. There we are, buying the presents *and* wrapping them, writing all the cards *and* posting them, while still trying to colour-coordinate the table decorations and produce perfectly piped pavlovas just like the ones we've seen in the glossy magazines, so that we can impress our guests.

Everything to do...

Martha was undoubtedly acting out of love—love for Jesus and his disciples—and focusing on trying to please them, ensuring that they enjoyed her hospitality. She must have wanted to put on a good spread for them, just as we would do for our families and friends at Christmas time. But she was also becoming annoyed, resentful and feeling that she had been left to do everything. She was doing the things that she felt she *should*, although her complaining tone and angry banging around in the kitchen could certainly have dampened the festivities.

We find that Martha's sister, Mary, all this time had, 'sat at the Lord's feet listening to what he said' (Luke 10:39). Mary's priorities were different. I'm sure the modern-day Mary would be as concerned as the 21st-century Martha that her family and friends were catered for at Christmas. But perhaps she would build her Christmas on a different foundation, with the baby Jesus and the Christmas story as her focus. Yes, her presents would be wrapped and her food prepared, but she'd make sure she had the time and energy to join in the real celebration.

Advertisements, television and magazines encourage us to demand perfection of ourselves—anything less and we have failed. Yet what if the perfectly piped pavlovas crumble in a heap or the beautifully arranged table is reduced to a sad, soggy mess by the first cup of juice that is spilt? What are we left with? Does it make our 'perfect' Christmas disintegrate too, leaving us with nothing but the taste of disappointment at our own inadequacies?

'Martha, Martha,' the Lord answered, 'you are worried and upset about many things, but only one thing is needed. Mary has chosen what is better, and it will not be taken away from her' (Luke 10:41–42).

The right choice

It is easy to find ourselves wrapped up in our worries at this time of year, upset by the 'shoulds' and the 'ought tos' as Martha was, caught up by the insatiable demands that perfection imposes upon us. But we do have a choice. We can allow ourselves to be tangled up in the mad hustle and bustle that surrounds us at this time of year, or we can stop. We can simply stop and ensure that we put at the centre of our focus the one important thing that cannot be taken away from us—Jesus.

Our modern Mary might overcook the turkey or drop the Christmas pudding, but I doubt that it would destroy her Christmas because her festivities are built on such firm foundations—the foundations of love, peace and joy gained from spending time with Jesus.

Will you take time to gaze into the manger this Christmas?

Sue Morton first began writing when she developed ME. She is married to Mark, an RAF air traffic controller, and they have four daughters.

Fog

Beryl Adamsbaum

Those of us who live in or near Geneva, Switzerland, spend part of each winter under a blanket of freezing, murky, damp fog. Outside of the relatively small 'Geneva basin', other people enjoy clear skies and warm sunshine. The word 'basin' explains it all: bad weather is funnelled to the Geneva end of the lake—Lac Léman or Lake Geneva—and hangs there. But the lake is not the only physical feature in the immediate area. Geneva is also surrounded by mountains—the Jura to the west; the Alps to the south-east; and two smaller nearby ranges, the Salève and the Voirons, across the border in France—all of which are made equally invisible by fog. Who, in their wildest imaginings, could ever visualize the breathtaking sight of Mont Blanc, rising to 4800 metres, its white peak etched against an intense blue sky? The fog completely obliterates all such beauty and majesty. However, that does not change the fact that, up there, and all around, the sun is shining! We know it is; we believe it is, even though we can't see it from down below.

Most of us who live in the area have been able, at one time or another, to drive the few kilometres needed in order to leave the cold, dark, clammy fog behind and enter a new world of light and warmth. What a contrast it is! We feel that we can really breathe again as we drink deeply of the fresh, clean air. We experience warmth as we lift our faces to the caressing rays of the sun. Our stiff, heavy limbs are invigorated as we step out freely and joyfully in the brightness.

Two worlds

It is like living in two different worlds—the disagreeable opaqueness 'down here', and the luminous transparency 'up there'. Doesn't that remind us of the spiritual reality that 'now we see through a glass, darkly; but then face to face' (1 Corinthians 13:12, AV)? Our lives on this earth are often clouded by fear, pain and uncertainty. At times we cannot perceive the love of God. We are blind to spiritual truths. We do not know which way to go. All seems dark. But, in spite of the dimness, God's promises remain true. We must hold on to them. After all, if we could see clearly at all times, what would be the point of faith? 'Faith is being... certain of what we do not see,' the writer of the letter to the Hebrews tells us (Hebrews 11:1, NIV). And the prophet Isaiah exhorts: 'Let him who walks in the dark, who has no light, trust in the name of the Lord and rely on his God' (Isaiah 50:10b, NIV). Even though difficulties and trials come our way and we often do not understand—we do not *see*—what is going on, we are already enjoying eternal life if we have entered into a relationship with God through Jesus Christ. Even in the midst of grief, we experience joy—the joy of sins forgiven and the assurance of spending eternity with our heavenly Father, 'in whose presence is fullness of joy'.

Next time the fog comes down, literally or figuratively, let us remember that there is sunlight and warmth beyond the greyness. And, in spite of the present reality, let us 'fix our eyes on Jesus', the one who is 'the light of the world'—'the bright and morning star', our Saviour.

Alarmed!

Chris Leonard

It's eleven at night and three-quarters of my beloved's body is hanging out of our bedroom window. He's utterly red in the face. I'm trying to convince myself that death by too much noise (as in Dorothy L. Sayers' victim-stuck-in-the-bell-tower murder mystery) is discredited by science as implausible. Nor is John likely to perish falling one storey on to our front lawn—break his back, maybe.

I notice a neighbour waving frantically and wonder if this heralds a road-wide protest riot. I can't hear a word she's saying, so I run downstairs and she bellows in my ear, 'We thought maybe you'd forgotten your alarm code.' No, we're not that dippy. When the thing started ringing all by itself we punched in the number countless times. Then John had the front of the control panel off. Tamper circuits, designed to defeat canny burglars, proved too efficient even for his wizardry with electronics. Those skills I trust, but not these acrobatics as he tries to reach the main wires and disconnect them from the bell. The inbuilt twenty-minute time-out silences it first. But the shame! We've joined the ranks of the accursed, whose burglar paranoia robs honest citizens of peace and sleep.

Prowlers

Don't you just hate alarms? Once we lived opposite a factory that installed a super-sensitive system. Every nocturnal prowler set it off—cats, foxes, even slugs, for all I knew. Once the initial bedlam stopped, squad cars would screech up and police vaulted the rattly gate, yards from our window, leaving their car radios victor-tangoing at full volume. Sleep deprivation fuelled my fury as I dragged my two pre-schoolers into the factory one morning, refusing to leave until I'd had a few choice words with the man in charge. However, the police's insistence that duty called them to catch cat-burglars, not mousing-moggies, plus their refusal to attend ever again, is what really spurred the factory management into solving the problem.

Soon afterwards I volunteered to work the occasional Saturday morning in a Christian bookshop run by my church. Previously it had been a jeweller's and its alarm proved fearsome. Even with it set to 'day time', tremor sensors designed to terrorize hardened smash-and-grabbers activated a deafening rumpus whenever a child, or adult, dropped anything on the wooden floor. I'd have to leave the till wide open, rush backstage to silence the wretched thing, and then pacify the screaming infants and frightened adults.

Surely the problem, the hub of the whole infuriating business, is that systems seldom catch real intruders but excel at false alarms, causing mayhem. It's a bit like me and worrying. I have this super-sensitive worry alarm which regularly keeps me awake at night, causing huge stress to friends, family and self—yet most of the time the worrying thing never happens. If it did, well, I know that God is my rock, my fortress. If he clothes the lilies and keeps an eye on the sparrows, how much more does he care for us humans. I'm aware that the Bible exhorts, 'Fear not' 365 times, one for every day of the year, and that Jesus advised us to take troubles one day at a time— yet I'm expert at projecting anxieties twenty years in advance. In fact, sometimes I wonder if all my close brushes with real burglar alarms haven't something to do with the sense of humour that God can use to get his truth home.

Gymnast?

You see, alarms dog me everywhere. When I hired our local library after hours to run a writing course, I found I had to lock and alarm the building on leaving at 10 p.m. I presented myself at the library one rainy Monday to find out how. It has two sets of sliding double doors. To exit, set both to 'open', punch numbers on to a pad and within seconds the alarm starts bleeping—alarmingly. Race to the doors, not forgetting to turn off the remaining light in the library itself, set the inner door to 'closed', while niftily stepping through it. Once it's shut, use the key with the red blob to lock it. Then operate the pull-cord of the porch light in the left hand and simultaneously turn the third, high-up key of the outer door to 'closed'. Before being trapped in the porch, hurl your body backwards into the dark and rain of the car park. This requires very long arms, no thought for personal safety, plus the reaction times and agility of an Olympic gymnast. As the alarm continues to bleep, lock the outer door with the last remaining key and twiddle a black button. It may (or may not) cause the bleeps to burst into a final triumphant tune and cease.

After an hour of providing the best afternoon's entertainment the library staff has ever enjoyed, I managed to blunder through these manoeuvres. Meanwhile, the library manager and I looked like drowned rats and readers grew ever more puzzled at being locked in the library or, worse, out in the rain. Some wondered why the assistant behind the counter had tears rolling down her cheeks. When I had to lock up for real, most of my writing group stayed behind to watch. It never failed to give them their best laugh of the week. I bet the Almighty was having a pretty good chuckle too, at me and all the worriers of this world. And I... well I had a whole new thing to worry about.

Words, words, words

Mary Reid

Have you ever been to a silent retreat? Many people find them a real blessing, but I have to confess that the first time I went to one, I found it almost impossible to be silent at the meal table. For me, to sit next to someone and not speak seems very strange. How do we get to know each other if we don't talk?

Words are an important part of our life, from babyhood onwards. I can remember the excitement when my first baby said 'da-da'. I was sure he was super-intelligent and speaking much earlier than all the other babies around. The fact that he said 'da-da' to everyone and everything, not just his daddy, was overlooked by this proud mother. I am now lapping up all the 'amazing' sentences of my youngest grandchild. 'Wherever did she learn that phrase from?' I marvel.

Words seem to have had quite an important place in my life, from the point of view of a teacher, an editor, a reluctant ladies' group speaker and, of course, as a normal human being. But for all of us, where would we be without words? We have words for speaking, for reading and writing, and we have the word of God.

Words to read

When I became a teacher, I soon discovered that the main activity of the day involved learning to read and write. As adults, we have forgotten what it is like to be a pre-schooler who has learned to talk but has not yet cottoned on to the link between the black squiggles on a page and the spoken word. I never cease to marvel at the fact that children do learn to read, some later than others. I used to keep a strip of Arabic script handy to show to impatient dads who couldn't see why their 5-year-old sons weren't reading yet. 'Would you read this to me, please?' I would ask sweetly.

I would have been floored if anyone had been able to read that script—but it usually made the point. To be able to link a particular squiggle to a sound, and then build a number of them into a word, is an amazing, God-given ability.

However, words aren't only there for us to read. Without words, we cannot get to know one another properly or understand what others think and feel and need. Communicating with other people, whether we are involved in discussing an important international issue or buying vegetables from the greengrocer, is a necessary skill. Have you ever been in a situation where everyone else is speaking a language you don't understand? They understand each other, but you can have no part in the conversation. I found myself in this situation once when I was emigrating to Canada—many years ago. I travelled on a Dutch vessel, and most of the other passengers and all the crew spoke Dutch. I felt more alone than if I had been on my own on that ship.

God's word

Being able to communicate with others through the spoken or written word is a learned skill, but it is also God's gift to his human creation. The Bible is referred to as 'the word of God', and it is through this amazing book that we know about God. We can read the stories of the kings and prophets in the Old Testament and about Jesus, his disciples and the early Church in the New Testament. But it is far more than a history book. It tells us how God has made himself known to his people. In the letter to the Hebrews (1:2–3) we learn that 'in the past God spoke to our ancestors many times and in many ways through the prophets, but in these last days he has spoken to us through his Son.' 'The Word,' John says at the beginning of his Gospel, 'became a human being and, full of grace and truth, lived among us' (1:14). With the coming of Jesus into our world, we know that his father is also our heavenly father, who loves us as his adopted children.

How would we know so much about Jesus if Matthew, Mark, Luke and John had not given us a permanent written record? From their Gospels we learn how Jesus treated people in need, how he healed those who were sick, what he taught his disciples about himself and how God wants us to live. They have given us this vivid word-picture of Jesus the man and Jesus the Son of God. John explains why he wrote his Gospel—'in order that you may believe that Jesus is the Messiah, the Son of God, and that through your faith in him you may have life' (John 20:31).

Our words

Matthew is the only one to write about an incident when some scribes and Pharisees actually said out loud that Jesus was an ally of the devil. Jesus reacted with righteous anger, saying, 'On the Judgment Day everyone will have to give account of every useless word they have ever spoken' (Matthew 12:36).

Now, we are never likely to say anything quite so wicked as that, but it's quite sobering to think that one day we will have to give an account to God for all our 'useless words'. James writes some strong things about the power of the tongue—the power of the words we say. 'No one has ever been able to tame the tongue… We use it to give thanks to our Lord and Father and also to curse our fellow man' (3:8–9). It is the words we use in our everyday lives that are so important—they become a window through which others can see what we are really like. If we are angry, our words will be angry; if we are unforgiving, others will see that through our speech. Perhaps we ought to follow the advice written in Proverbs 10:19: 'The more you talk the more likely you are to sin. If you are wise you will keep quiet'!

Once I start reading the book of Proverbs, I am hooked—it is full of gems of wisdom and common sense. 'What a joy it is to find just the right word for the right occasion!' (15:23). 'Kind words are like honey—sweet to the taste and good for your health' (16:24). 'Thoughtless words can wound as deeply as any sword, but wisely spoken words can heal' (12:18).

In conclusion

With words we learn about each other. Through Jesus, the Word of God, we have eternal life. And it is through the way we speak and the words we use in our everyday life that we can reflect God's love to those around us.

An extract from
Quiet Spaces

Patricia Wilson

In today's world, women are busier than ever. Not only does a woman often manage the multiple tasks and responsibilities of home, family, and career, but she also juggles a variety of roles—mother, daughter, wife, employee, friend, volunteer—the list seems endless. Each morning she hits the ground running, to-do list in hand and pocket planner held aloft. By the time the last minutes of the day drain away, she falls into an exhausted sleep, haunted by the ghosts of things yet to do.

How can a busy woman find time for personal prayer during one hectic day after another? How can God speak to her amid the turbulence of timetables, schedules and agendas? Where is a moment for her to hear God's still small voice above the tumult?

Is this your challenge—finding time to pray? Believe it or not, time for prayer is available to you through the Bowling Ball Solution.

Imagine that your day is like an empty cardboard box about two feet square. This box contains all the waking time available to you in a day. Your most important to-do items—writing a business report, going to the doctor, meeting with your child's teacher, shopping for the week's groceries—are like bowling balls. They are large, bulky, inflexible blocks of time.

How many of these will fit into your box? About four? Now your day is full of important things to do.

What about the spaces between the bowling balls? You have room for a few tennis balls—things that take a little less time than your major projects but still have to get done: returning a library book, dropping off the dry cleaning, picking up milk on the way home. These tennis balls of time soon fill up the spaces around your bowling balls.

A little space remains, however. You can put in a few golf balls—

those unplanned half hours of time here and there when meetings start late, new work comes in, or a meeting runs overtime.

Your time box is now full. There's no room for anything else, much less room for your personal prayer time!

Now in your mind's eye see grains of sand. How many you can pour into the box before it's completely filled? Quite a few!

The grains of sand are stray minutes of unassigned time. They usually go unnoticed and unused. Where do they come from?

You can find these stray minutes while you are on hold with that council department, sitting in the dentist's waiting-room, stopped in a traffic jam, on a short coffee break, waiting for a meeting to begin, between phone calls—in any one of the myriad times during the day when a small opportunity of time opens up. These 'quiet spaces' are all around you.

Quiet Spaces is a book of just such times—short interludes of time as little as five minutes each—that you can capture and use to touch the hand of God...

Whenever you have a Quiet Space, take the opportunity to spend those few minutes with God. Read through the passage from Psalms (under Calming) three times, which will help calm your mind and heart. If you wish, you may write the psalm on an index card and leave it where it you can see it during the day.

Next, focus your thoughts with a moment of imagination. The Centring suggestions will give you an idea of how to do this. You don't have to close your eyes.

Now read through the short prayer. Read it slowly, paying attention to the words. The short sentences and thoughts of Quiet Space prayers help you do this. If you find your mind wandering, start over at the beginning and read through again. Where you see italicized words in the prayer, substitute the name, gender, or situation of your own personal prayer.

When you finish the prayer, read the words of Jesus (under Listening). Consider how they relate to your life and your present situation. Quietly thank Jesus for his love and care.

Then anchor your experience and prepare to return to your world by using the Returning exercise. Sometimes you can continue to use this exercise throughout the day to remind you of the Quiet Space...

This book contains many Quiet Spaces, divided into various prayer subjects. Whether you choose to read them in sequence, randomly, or by topic, God is waiting to speak to you in the Quiet Space.

✣

CELEBRATING CHRISTMAS

CALMING

When I look at your heavens,
the work of your fingers,
the moon and the stars that you have established,
what are human beings that you
are mindful of them,
mortals that you care for them?

Psalm 8:3–4 (NRSV)

CENTRING

Imagine standing alone on a hillside at night. The sky is filled with stars. Suddenly one star glows brightly, increasing in radiance until you feel bathed in its light. With this starlight comes a profound sense of peace and joy.

PRAYING

Christmas is such a wonderful time, Jesus, when we celebrate your birth into our dark world.

Christmas is also a difficult time. Many people don't have the trappings of the season: the family, the feasting, the gifts, the social whirl.

It's difficult, Jesus, when I suddenly discover that I'm just like everyone else:

rushing,

finding,

doing,

eating,

drinking,

and forgetting why I celebrate Christmas.

It's difficult because everything around me pushes me into the Christmas of this world.

Even at church I feel a sense of rushing that has nothing in common with the peace and serenity of Christmas.

The Sunday school plays,
    the Christmas bazaar,
        the choir concerts,
            the special services,
all hurl me toward Christmas Day.

Then when the day finally arrives, I'm too tired to think about the reason I'm celebrating. Once the presents have been unwrapped, food has been devoured, and families have been duly visited, not much time remains for you.

And so, Jesus, I'm asking you for a special gift as I celebrate your birth. Pour down the light of your star in the East. Bathe me in its peaceful light so that I can experience profound joy, which comes from knowing that my Saviour is born. Blessed Jesus, keep me in your peace, today and always.

LISTENING

I have come that they may have life, and have it to the full.

John 10:10

RETURNING

As you prepare for Christmas Day, every time you feel yourself beginning to get caught up in this world's Christmas or beginning to feel stressed or hurried, take a moment to close your eyes briefly and remember the beautiful, brightly shining star. Allow its light to pour down upon you. Feel the peace, experience the joy, and celebrate the birth of your Saviour.

Other Christina Press titles

Who'd Plant a Church? Diana Archer
£5.99 in UK

Planting an Anglican church from scratch, with a team of four—two adults and two children—is an unusual adventure even in these days. Diana Archer is a vicar's wife who gives a distinctive perspective on parish life.

Pathway Through Grief edited by Jean Watson
£6.99 in UK

Ten Christians, each bereaved, share their experience of loss. Frank and sensitive accounts offering comfort and reassurance to those recently bereaved. Jean Watson has lost her own husband and believes that those involved in counselling will also gain new insights from these honest personal chronicles.

God's Catalyst Rosemary Green
£8.99 in UK

Rosemary Green's international counselling ministry has prayer and listening to God at its heart. Changed lives and rekindled faith testify to God's healing power. Here she provides insight, inspiration and advice for both counsellors and concerned Christians who long to be channels of God's Spirit to help those in need. *God's Catalyst* is a unique tool for the non-specialist counsellor; for the pastor who has no training; for the Christian who wants to come alongside hurting friends.

Angels Keep Watch Carol Hathorne
£5.99 in UK

A true adventure showing how God still directs our lives,not with wind, earthquake or fire, but by the still, small voice.

'Go to Africa.' The Lord had been saying it for over forty years. At last, Carol Hathorne had obeyed, going out to Kenya with her husband. On the eastern side of Nairobi, where tourists never go, they came face to face with dangers, hardships and poverty on a daily basis, but experienced the joy of learning that Christianity is still growing in God's world.

Not a Super-Saint Liz Hansford
£6.99 in UK

'You might have thought Adrian Plass... had cornered the market in amusing diary writing. Well, check out Liz Hansford's often hilarious account of life as a Baptist minister's wife in Belfast. Highly recommended.' *The New Christian Herald*

Liz Hansford describes the outlandish situations which arise in the Manse, where life is both fraught and tremendous fun. *Not a Super-Saint* is for the ordinary Christian who feels they must be the only one who hasn't quite got it all together.

The Addiction of a Busy Life Edward England
£5.99 in UK

Twelve lessons from a devastating heart attack. Edward, a giant of Christian publishing in the UK, and founder of Christina Press, shares what the Lord taught him when his life nearly came to an abrupt end. Although not strictly a Christina title (Edward lacks the gender qualifications), we believe you may want to buy this for the busy men in your lives.

'A wonderful story of success and frailty, of love and suffering, of despair and hope. If you are too busy to read this book, you are too busy.' *Dr Michael Green*

Life Path Luci Shaw
£5.99 in UK

Personal and spiritual growth through journal writing. Life has a way of slipping out of the back door while we're not looking. Keeping a journal can enrich life as we live it, and bring it all back later. Luci Shaw shows how a journal can also help us grow in our walk with God.

Precious to God Sarah Bowen
£5.99 in UK

Two young people, delighted to be starting a family, have their expectations shattered by the arrival of a handicapped child. And yet this is only the first of many difficulties to be faced. What was initially a tragedy is, through faith, transformed into a story of inspiration, hope and spiritual enrichment.

All the above titles are available from Christian bookshops everywhere, or in case of difficulty, direct from Christina Press using the order form on page 156.

Other BRF titles

Living the Gospel Helen Julian CSF
The spirituality of St Francis and St Clare
£5.99 in UK

Finding freedom in simplicity and voluntary poverty, living in harmony with creation, seeking to be a brother to everyone and everything—so much of the teaching of St Francis directly challenges the values of today's consumer-driven culture, providing a radical, liberating alternative. Yet while he remains an enduringly popular figure in the history of Christian spirituality, St Clare is far less well-known.

Living the Gospel looks at St Francis and St Clare together, showing how they shared responsibility for the growth and influence of the Franciscan order, and how deeply rooted their teaching was in scripture.

This book is ideal for people already interested in the teaching of St Francis, and it introduces St Clare to a wider audience—a comparatively little-known but surprisingly influential female spiritual leader.

The Gifts of Baptism Margaret Withers
An essential guide for parents, sponsors and leaders
£4.99 in UK

A child is going to be baptized. Through baptism we become members of God's family, the Church. Preparing to take part in this great event will include exploring some of the things that make up the baptismal service. You may be the child's parent, or you may be a godparent or sponsor. Perhaps you are a church leader looking for material to use as a preparation course for a group of parents. Or you may be talking to children who are going to be present at a baptism.

This book takes you through the service by following the journey of a young child and his baby sister as they prepare to be baptized. Each chapter introduces and discusses the signs and symbols used, alongside some of the text and prayers. It also uses short extracts from the Bible to describe the ways that people have seen themselves as belonging to God, their creator, and the new life that Jesus promises to all who follow him.

Lighted Windows Margaret Silf
An Advent calendar for a world in waiting
£6.99 in UK

The birth of a baby invariably stirs deep wells of hope in the human heart. Perhaps in this generation, things will get better. Perhaps this child will make a difference.

As we approach the Christmas season, we prepare to celebrate the coming to earth of someone who really does make a difference. At this season the 'windows' of our human experience can change from rows of faceless panes, perhaps grimy with dirt, into lighted windows that open up new possibilities and coax us into a place where rejoicing might be possible.

The journey mapped out in this book is an invitation to look into some of these lighted windows, and discover a few reflections of what we wait for, and long for—reflections of God's guidance, his call to trust him and live by his wisdom.

Colours of God Diana Murrie
A book of reflective words and activities exploring the gift of colour in everyday life
£5.99 in UK

We sometimes take for granted the colours all around us. We look… but we do not see.

This book can help us look and see, perhaps, in a different way. It is an invitation to discover some new exciting ideas about colour, and to think, reflect and wonder afresh at things we knew before. It is designed to help teachers looking for resources in a primary school or a church, for parents, grandparents or godparents looking for a suitable gift for a child, or for children to read by themselves or share with someone else.

There are lots of wondering questions and fascinating ideas, facts and activites to explore as we think about the myriad of colour God has given us to enjoy.

This is an unusual book. Even though it is called *Colours of God*, there are no colours in it! They are in our minds, our memories and in the world all around us, just waiting for us to discover for ourselves!

All the above titles are available from Christian bookshops everywhere or, in case of difficulty, direct from BRF using the order form on page 157.

Christina Press Publications Order Form

All of these publications are available from Christian bookshops everywhere or, in case of difficulty, direct from the publisher. Please make your selection below, complete the payment details and send your order with payment as appropriate to:

Christina Press Ltd, 17 Church Road, Tunbridge Wells, Kent TN1 1LG

		Qty	Price	Total
8700	God's Catalyst	_____	£8.99	_____
8702	Precious to God	_____	£5.99	_____
8703	Angels Keep Watch	_____	£5.99	_____
8704	Life Path	_____	£5.99	_____
8705	Pathway Through Grief	_____	£6.99	_____
8706	Who'd Plant a Church?	_____	£5.99	_____
8708	Not a Super-Saint	_____	£6.99	_____
8705	The Addiction of a Busy Life	_____	£5.99	_____

POSTAGE AND PACKING CHARGES				
	UK	Europe	Surface	Air Mail
£7.00 & under	£1.25	£2.25	£2.25	£3.50
£7.10–£29.99	£2.25	£5.50	£7.50	£11.00
£30.00 & over	free	prices on request		

Total cost of books   £ _____
Postage and Packing   £ _____
TOTAL   £ _____

All prices are correct at time of going to press, are subject to the prevailing rate of VAT and may be subject to change without prior warning.

Name _____

Address _____

_____

_____ Postcode _____

Total enclosed £ _____ (cheques should be made payable to 'Christina Press Ltd')

 Please send me further information about Christina Press publications

DBDWG0303

BRF Publications Order Form

All of these publications are available from Christian bookshops everywhere, or in case of difficulty direct from the publisher. Please make your selection below, complete the payment details and send your order with payment as appropriate to:

BRF, First Floor, Elsfield Hall, 15–17 Elsfield Way, Oxford OX2 8FG

		Qty	Price	Total
124 X	Beauty from Ashes	____	£5.99	____
126 6	Living the Gospel	____	£5.99	____
136 3	The Heart of Christmas	____	£5.99	____
208 4	The Gifts of Baprism	____	£4.99	____
240 8	Colours of God	____	£5.99	____
255 6	Lighted Windows	____	£6.99	____

POSTAGE AND PACKING CHARGES				
	UK	Europe	Surface	Air Mail
£7.00 & under	£1.25	£3.00	£3.50	£5.50
£7.10–£29.99	£2.25	£5.50	£6.50	£10.00
£30.00 & over	free	prices on request		

Total cost of books £ _____

Postage and Packing £ _____

TOTAL £ _____

All prices are correct at time of going to press, are subject to the prevailing rate of VAT and may be subject to change without prior warning.

Name _____

Address _____

_____ Postcode _____

Total enclosed £ _____ (cheques should be made payable to 'BRF')

Payment by: cheque ❏ postal order ❏ Visa ❏ Mastercard ❏ Switch ❏

Card no. ☐☐☐☐ ☐☐☐☐ ☐☐☐☐ ☐☐☐☐ ☐☐☐☐

Card expiry date ☐☐☐☐ Issue number (Switch) ☐☐☐☐

Signature _____

(essential if paying by credit/Switch card)

❏ Please do not send me further information about BRF publications

Visit the BRF website at www.brf.org.uk

Subscription Information

Each issue of *Day by Day with God* is available from Christian book-shops everywhere. Copies may also be available through your church Book Agent or from the person who distributes Bible reading notes in your church.

Alternatively you may obtain *Day by Day with God* on subscription direct from the publishers. There are two kinds of subscription:

Individual Subscriptions are for four copies or less, and include postage and packing. To order an annual Individual Subscription please complete the details on page 160 and send the coupon with payment to BRF in Oxford. You can also use the form to order a Gift Subscription for a friend.

Church Subscriptions are for five copies or more, sent to one address, and are supplied post free. Church Subscriptions run from 1 May to 30 April each year and are invoiced annually. To order a Church Subscription please complete the details opposite and send the coupon to BRF in Oxford. You will receive an invoice with the first issue of notes.

All subscription enquiries should be directed to:

BRF
First Floor
Elsfield Hall
15–17 Elsfield Way
Oxford
OX2 8FG

Tel: 01865 319700
Fax: 01865 319701
E-mail: subscriptions@brf.org.uk

Church Subscriptions

The Church Subscription rate for *Day by Day with God* will be £10.20 per person until April 2004.

☐ I would like to take out a church subscription for _____ (Qty) copies.

☐ Please start my order with the January / May / September 2004* issue.
I would like to pay annually/receive an invoice with each edition of the notes*.
(*Please delete as appropriate)

Please do not send any money with your order. Send your order to BRF and we will send you an invoice. The Church Subscription year is from May to April. If you start subscribing in the middle of a subscription year we will invoice you for the remaining number of issues left in that year.

Name and address of the person organising the Church Subscription:

Name _____

Address _____

_____

Postcode _____ Telephone _____

Church _____

Name of Minister _____

Name and address of the person paying the invoice if the invoice needs to be sent directly to them:

Name _____

Address _____

_____

Postcode _____ Telephone _____

Please send your coupon to:

BRF
First Floor
Elsfield Hall
15–17 Elsfield Way
Oxford
OX2 8FG

☐ Please do not send me further information about BRF publications

DBDWG0303   BRF is a Registered Charity

Individual Subscriptions

☐ I would like to give a gift subscription (please complete both name and address sections below)

☐ I would like to take out a subscription myself (complete name and address details only once)

The completed coupon should be sent with appropriate payment to BRF. Alternatively, please write to us quoting your name, address, the subscription you would like for either yourself or a friend (with their name and address), the start date and credit card number, expiry date and signature if paying by credit card.

Gift subscription name _____

Gift subscription address _____

_____ Postcode_____

Please send to the above for one year, beginning with the January / May / September 2004 issue: (delete as applicable)

	UK	Surface	Air Mail
Day by Day with God	☐ £12.15	☐ £13.50	☐ £15.75
2-year subscription	☐ £20.40	N/A	N/A

Please complete the payment details below and send your coupon, with appropriate payment, to BRF, First Floor, Elsfield Hall, 15–17 Elsfield Way, Oxford OX2 8FG

Your name _____

Your address _____

_____ Postcode_____

Total enclosed £ _____ (cheques should be made payable to 'BRF')

Payment by: cheque ☐ postal order ☐ Visa ☐ Mastercard ☐ Switch ☐

Card no. ☐☐☐☐☐☐☐☐☐☐☐☐☐☐☐☐☐☐☐

Card expiry date ☐☐☐☐   Issue number (Switch) ☐☐☐☐

Signature _____

(essential if paying by credit/Switch card)

NB: These notes are also available from Christian bookshops everywhere.

☐ Please do not send me further information about BRF publications

DBDWG0303   BRF is a Registered Charity